FABRE

Poet of Science

FABRE,
Poet of Science

G. V. LEGROS

Translated by
BERNARD MIALL

Preface by
J. H. FABRE

HORIZON PRESS   NEW YORK

PREFACE

THE good friend who has so successfully terminated the task which he felt a vocation to undertake thought it would be of advantage to complete it by presenting to the reader a picture both of my life as a whole and of the work which it has been given me to accomplish.

The better to accomplish his undertaking, he abstracted from my correspondence, as well as from the long conversations which we have so often enjoyed together, a great number of those memories of varying importance which serve as landmarks in life ; above all in a life like mine, not exempt from many cares, yet not very fruitful in incidents or great vicissitudes, since it has been passed very largely, in especial during the last thirty years, in the most absolute retirement and the completest silence.

Moreover, it was not unimportant to warn the public against the errors, exaggerations, and legends which have collected about my person, and thus to set all things in their true light.

In undertaking this task my devoted disciple has to some extent been able to replace those *Memoirs* which he suggested that I should write, and which only my bad health has prevented me from undertaking; for I feel that henceforth I am done with wide horizons and "far-reaching thoughts."

And yet on reading now the old letters which he has exhumed from a mass of old yellow papers, and which he has presented and co-ordinated with so pious a care, it seems to me that in the depths of my being I can still feel rising in me all the fever of my early years, all the enthusiasm of long ago, and that I should still be no less ardent a worker were not the weakness of my eyes and the failure of my strength to-day an insurmountable obstacle.

Thoroughly grasping the fact that one cannot write a biography without entering into the sphere of those ideas which alone make a life interesting, he has revived around me that world which I have so long contemplated, and summarized in a striking epitome, and as a strict interpreter, my methods (which are, as will be seen,

within the reach of all), my ideas, and the whole
body of my works and discoveries ; and despite
the obvious difficulty which such an attempt
would appear to present, he has succeeded most
wonderfully in achieving the most lucid, complete, and vital exposition of these matters that
I could possibly have wished.

J. H. FABRE.

SÉRIGNAN, VAUCLUSE,
November 12, 1911.

CONTENTS

INTRODUCTION

HERE I offer to the public the life of Jean-Henri Fabre; at once an admiring commentary upon his work and an act of pious homage, such as ought to be offered, while he lives, to the great naturalist who is even to-day so little known.

Hitherto it was not easy to speak of Henri Fabre with exactitude. An enemy to all advertisement, he has so discreetly held himself withdrawn that one might almost say that he has encouraged, by his silence, many doubtful or unfounded rumours, which in course of time would become even more incorrect.

For example, although quite recently his material situation was presented in the gloomiest of lights, while it had really for some time ceased to be precarious, it is none the less true that during his whole life he has had to labour prodigiously in order to earn a little money to feed and rear his family, to the great detriment of his scientific inquiries; and we cannot but regret that he was not freed from all material cares at least twenty years earlier than was the case.

But he was not one to speak of his troubles to the first comer ; and it was only after the sixth volume of the *Souvenirs entomologiques* had appeared that his reserve was somewhat miti-gated. Yet it was necessary that he should speak of these troubles, that he should tell everything ; and, thanks to his conversation and his letters, I have been able to revive the past.

Among the greatest of my pleasures I count the notable honour of having known him, and intimately. As an absorbed and attentive witness I was present at the accomplishment of his last labours ; I watched his last years of work, so critical, so touching, so forsaken, before his ultimate resurrection. What fruitful and sug-gestive lessons I learned in his company, as we paced the winding paths of his Harmas ; or while I sat beside him, at his patriarchal table, interro-gating that memory of his, so rich in remem-brances that even the remotest events of his life were as near to him as those that had only then befallen him ; so that the majority of the judg-ments to be found in this book, of which not a line has been written without his approval, may be regarded as the direct emanation of his mind.

As far as possible I have allowed him to speak

himself. Has he not sketched the finest pages of
his " biography of a solitary student " in those
racy chapters of his *Souvenirs* : those in which
he has developed his genesis as a naturalist and
the history of the evolution of his ideas? [1]   In
all cases I have only introduced such indications
as were essential to complete the sequence of
events.   It would have been idle to re-tell in
the same terms what every one may read elsewhere, or to repeat in different and less happy
terms what Fabre himself has told so well.

I have therefore applied myself more especially to filling the gaps which he has left, by
listening to his conversation, by appealing to
his memories, by questioning his contemporaries,
by recording the impressions of his sometime
pupils.   I have endeavoured to assemble all these
data, in order to authenticate them, and have
also gleaned many facts among his manuscripts,[2]
and have had recourse to all that portion of his
correspondence which fortunately fell into my
hands.

This correspondence, to be truthful, does not
appear at any time to have been very assiduous.
Fabre, as we shall see in the story of his life,[3]
disliked writing letters, both in his studious youth
and during the later period of isolation and
silence.

On the other hand, although he wrote but little, he never wrote with difficulty or as a mere matter of duty. Among all the letters which I have succeeded in collecting there are scarcely any that are not of interest from one point of view or another. No frivolous narratives, no futile acquaintances, no commonplace intimacies; everything in his life is serious, and everything makes for a goal.

But we must set apart, as surpassing all others in interest, the letters which Fabre addressed to his brother during the years spent as school-master at Carpentras or Ajaccio; for these are more especially instructive in respect of the almost unknown years of his youth; these most of all reveal his personality and are one of the finest illustrations that could be given of his life, a true poem of energy and disinterested labour.

I have to thank M. Frédéric Fabre, who, in his fraternal piety, has generously placed all his family records at my disposal, and also his two sons, my dear friends Antonin Fabre, councillor at the Court of Nîmes, and Henri Fabre, of Avignon, for these precious documents; and I take this opportunity of expressing my profound gratitude.

Let me at the same time thank all those who

have associated themselves with my efforts by supplying me with letters in their possession and furnishing me with personal information ; and in particular Mme Henry Devillario, M. Achard, and M. J. Belleudy, ex-prefect of Vaucluse ; not forgetting M. Louis Charrasse, teacher at Beaumont-d'Orange, and M. Vayssières, professor of the Faculty of Sciences at Marseilles, all of whom I have to thank for personal and intimate information.

I must also express my gratitude to M. Henri Bergson, Professor Bouvier, and the learned M. Paul Marchal for the advice and the valuable suggestions which they offered me during the preparation of this book.

I shall feel fully repaid for my pains if this *Life* of one of the greatest of the world's naturalists, by enabling men to know him better, also leads them to love him the more.

FABRE, POET OF SCIENCE

I

THE INTUITION OF NATURE

EACH thing created, says Emerson, has its painter or its poet. Like the enchanted princess of the fairy-tales, it awaits its predestined liberator.

Every part of nature has its mystery, and its beauty, its logic and its explanation ; and the epigraph given me by Fabre himself, which appears on the title-page of this volume, is in no way deceptive. The tiny insects buried in the soil or creeping over leaf or blade have for him been sufficient to evoke the most important, the most fascinating problems, and have revealed a whole world of miracle and poetry.

He saw the light at Saint-Léons, a little commune of the canton of Vezins in the Haut Rouergue, on the 22nd December, 1823, some seven years earlier than Mistral, his most famous neighbour, the greater lustre of whose celebrity was to eclipse his own.

Here he essayed his earliest steps ; here he stammered his first syllables.

His early childhood, however, was passed almost wholly at Malaval, a tiny hamlet in the parish of Lavaysse, whose belfry was visible at quite a short distance ; but to reach it one had to travel nearly twenty-five rough, mountainous miles, through a whole green countryside ; green, but bare, and lacking in charm.[1]

All his paternal forbears came from Malaval, and thence one day his father, Antoine Fabre, came to dwell at Saint-Léons, as a consequence of his marriage with the daughter of the *huissier*, Victoire Salgues, and in order to prepare himself, as working apprentice, in the tricks and quibbles of the law.[2]

In the roads of Malaval, bordered with brambles, in the glades of bracken, and amid the meadows of broom, he received his first impressions of nature. At Malaval too lived his grandmother, the good old woman who could lull him to sleep at night with beautiful stories and simple legends, while she wound her distaff or span her bobbin.

But what were all these imaginary marvels, what were the ogres who smelt fresh meat, or

" the fairies who turned pumpkins into coaches and lizards into footmen " beside all the marvels of reality, which already he was beginning to perceive?

For above all things he was born a poet: a poet by instinct and by vocation. From his earliest childhood, " the brain hardly released from the swaddling-bands of unconsciousness," the things of the outer world left a profound and living impression. As far back as he can remember, while still quite a child, " a little monkey of six, still dressed in a little baize frock," or just " wearing his first braces," he sees himself " in ecstasy before the splendours of the wing-cases of a gardener-beetle, or the wings of a butter-fly." At nightfall, among the bushes, he learned to recognize the chirp of the grasshopper. To put it in his own words, " he made for the flowers and insects as the Pieris makes for the cabbage and the Vanessa makes for the nettle." The riches of the rocks; the life which swarms in the depth of the waters; the world of plants and animals, that " prodigious poem; all nature filled him with curiosity and wonder." " A voice charmed him; untranslatable; sweeter than language and vague as a dream." 3

These peculiarities are all the more astonishing

in that they seem to be absolutely spontaneous and in nowise hereditary. What his parents were he himself has told us : small farmers, cultivating a little unprofitable land ; poor " husbandmen, sowers of rye, cowherds " ; and in the wretched surroundings of his childhood, when the only light, of an evening, came from a splinter of pine, steeped in resin, which was held by a strip of slate stuck into the wall ; when his folk shut themselves in the byre, in times of severe cold, to save a little firewood and while away the evenings ; when close at hand, through the bitter wind, they heard the howling of the wolves : here, it would seem, was nothing propitious to the birth of such tastes, if he had not borne them naturally within him.

But is it not the very essence of genius, as it is the peculiarity of instinct, to spring from the depths of the invisible?

Yet who shall say what stores of thought unspoken, what unknown treasures of observation never to be communicated, what patient reflections unuttered, may be housed in those toil-worn brains, in which, perhaps, slowly and obscurely, accumulate the germs of faculties and talents by which some more favoured descendant may one day benefit? How many poets have

died unpublished or unperceived, in whom only
the power of expression was lacking !

When he was seven years old his parents
recalled him to Saint-Léons, in order to send
him to the school kept by his godfather, Pierre
Ricard, the village schoolmaster, " at once
barber, bellringer, and singer in the choir."
Rembrandt, Teniers, nor Van Ostade never
painted anything more picturesque than the
room which served at the same time as kitchen,
refectory, and bedroom, with " halfpenny prints
papering the walls " and " a huge chimney, for
which each had to bring his log of a morning
in order to enjoy the right to a place at the
fireside."

He was never to forget these beloved places,
blessed scenes of his childhood, amid which he
grew up like a little savage, and through all
his material sufferings, all his hours of bitterness, and even in the resignation of age, their
idyllic memory sufficed to make his life fragrant.
He would always see the humble paternal garden,
the brook where he used to surprise the cray-
fish, the ash-tree in which he found his first
goldfinch's nest, and " the flat stone on which
he heard, for the first time, the mellow ringing

of the bellringer frog." 4   Later, when writing
to his brother, he was to recall the good days
of still careless life, when " he would sprawl, the
sun on his belly, on the mosses of the wood of
Vezins, eating his black bread and cream " or
" ring the bells of Saint-Léons " and " pull the
tails of the bulls of Lavaysse." 5

For Henri had a brother, Frédéric, barely two
years younger than he ; equally meditative by
nature, and of a serious, upright mind ; but his
tastes inclined rather to matters of administration
and the understanding of business, so that where
Frédéric was bored, Henri was more than content, thirstily drinking in science and poetry
" among the blue campanulas of the hills, the
pink heather of the mountains, the golden butter-
cups of the meadows, and the odorous bracken
of the woods." 6   Apart from this the two
brothers " were one " ; they understood one
another in a marvellous fashion, and always loved
one another.   Henri never failed to watch over
Frédéric with a wholly fatherly solicitude ; he
was prodigal of advice, helpful with his experience, doing his best to smooth away all
difficulties, encouraging him to walk in his foot-
steps and make his way through the world behind
him.   He was his confidant, giving an ear to

all that befell him of good or ill ; to his fears,
his disappointments, his hopes, and all his
thoughts ; and he took the keenest interest in
his studies and researches.   On the other hand,
he had no more sure and devoted friend ; none
more proud of his first success, and in later days
no more enthusiastic admirer, and none more
eager for his fame.[7]

He was twelve years old when his father,
" the first of all his line, was tempted by the
town," and led all his family to Rodez, there to
keep a café.   The future naturalist entered the
school of this town, where he served Mass on
Sunday, in the chapel, in order to pay his fees.
There again he was interested in the animal
creation above all.   When he began to construe
Virgil the only thing that charmed him, and
which he remembered, was the landscape in
which the persons of the poem move, in which
are so many " exquisite details concerning the
cicada, the goat, and the laburnum."

Thus four more years went by : but then his
parents were constrained to seek their fortune
elsewhere, and transported their household to
Toulouse, where again the father kept a café.
The young Henri was admitted gratuitously to
the seminary of the Esquille, where he managed

to complete his fifth year. Unfortunately his progress was soon interrupted by a new exodus on the part of his family, which emigrated this time to Montpellier, where he was haunted for a time by dreams of medicine, to which he seemed notably adapted. Finally, a run of bad luck persisting, he had to bid farewell to his studies and gain his bread as best he could. We see him set out along the wide white roads : lost, almost a wanderer, seeking his living by the sweat of his brow ; one day selling lemons at the fair of Beaucaire, under the arcades of the market or before the barracks of the Pré ; another day enlisting in a gang of labourers who were working on the line from Beaucaire to Nîmes, which was then in process of construction. He knew gloomy days, lonely and despairing. What was he doing? of what was he dreaming? The love of nature and the passion for learning sustained him in spite of all, and often served him as nourishment ; as on the day when he dined on a few grapes, plucked furtively at the edge of a field, after exchanging the poor remnant of his last halfpence for a little volume of Reboul's poems ; soothing his hunger by reciting the verses of the gentle baker-poet. Often some creature kept him company ; some insect never seen before was often his greatest pleasure; such as the pine-chafer, which he encountered then for the first time; that superb beetle, whose black or chestnut coat is sprinkled with specks of white velvet; which squeaks when captured, emitting a slight complaining sound, like the vibration of a pane of glass rubbed with the tip of a moistened finger.[8]

Already this young mind, romantic and classic at once, full of the ideal, and so positive that it seemed to seek support in an intense grasp of things and beings—two gifts well-nigh incompatible, and often mutually destructive—already it knew, not only the love of study and a passion for the truth, but the sovereign delight of feeling everything and understanding everything.

It was under these conditions—that is, amid the rudest privations—that he ventured to enter a competitive examination for a bursary at the École Normale Primaire of Avignon; and his will-power realized this first miracle of his career —he straightway obtained the highest place.

In those days, when education had barely reached the lower classes, the instruction given in the primary normal school was still of the most summary. Spelling, arithmetic, and geometry practically exhausted its resources. As for

natural history, a poor despised science, almost
unknown, no one dreamed of it, and no one
learned or taught it; the syllabus ignored
it, because it led to nothing. For Fabre
only, notwithstanding, it was his fixed idea, his
constant preoccupation, and " while the dictation
class was busy around him, he would examine,
in the secrecy of his desk, the sting of a wasp
or the fruit of the oleander," and intoxicate
himself with poetry.[9] His pedagogic studies
suffered thereby, and the first part of his stay
at the normal school was by no means extremely
brilliant. In the middle of his second year he
was declared idle, and even marked as an insufficient pupil and of mediocre intelligence. Stung
to the quick, he begged as a favour that he
should be given the opportunity of following the
third year's course in the six months that
remained, and he made such an effort that at the
end of the year he victoriously won his superior
certificate.[10]

A year in advance of the regulation studies,
his curiosity might now exercise itself freely in
every direction, and little by little it became
universal. A chance chemistry lesson finally
awakened in him the appetite for knowledge,
the passion for all the sciences, of which he
thirsted to know at least the elements. Between

whiles he returned to his Latin, translating
Horace and re-reading Virgil. One day his
director put an *Imitation* into his hands, with
double columns in Greek and Latin. The latter,
which he knew fairly well, assisted him to
decipher the Greek. He hastened to commit to
memory the vocables, and idioms and phrases of
all kinds,[11] and in this curious fashion he learned
the language. This was his only method of learning languages. It is the process which he re-
commended to his brother, who was commencing
Latin :

" Take Virgil, a dictionary, and a grammar,
and translate from Latin into French for ever and
for ever ; to make a good version you need only
common sense and very little grammatical knowledge or other pedantic accessories.

" Imagine an old inscription half-effaced :
correctness of judgment partly supplies the
missing words, and the sense appears as if the
whole were legible. Latin, for you, is the old
inscription ; the root of the word alone is
legible : the veil of an unknown language hides
the value of the termination : you have only the
half of the words ; but you have common sense
too, and you will make use of it." [12]

II

THE PRIMARY TEACHER

FURNISHED with his superior diploma, he left
the normal school at the age of nineteen, and
commenced as a primary teacher in the College
of Carpentras.

The salary of the school teacher, in the year
1842, did not exceed £28 a year, and this ungrateful calling barely fed him, save on " chick-
peas and a little wine." But we must beware lest,
in view of the increasing and excessive dearness
of living in France, the beggarly salaries of the
poor schoolmasters of a former day, so little
worthy of their labours and their social utility,
appear even more disproportionately small than
they actually were. What is more to the point,
the teachers had no pension to hope for. They
could only count on a perpetuity of labour, and
when sickness or infirmity arrived, when old age
surprised them, after fifty or sixty years of a
narrow and precarious existence, it was not

merely poverty that awaited them; for many there was nothing but the blackest destitution. A little later, when they began to entertain a vague hope of deliverance, the retiring pension which was held up to their gaze, in the distant future, was at first no more than forty francs, and they had to await the advent of Duruy, the great minister and liberator, before primary instruction was in some degree raised from this ignominious level of abasement.

It was a melancholy place, this college, " where life had something cloistral about it : each master occupied two cells, for, in considera- tion of a modest payment, the majority were lodged in the establishment, and ate in com- mon at the principal's table."

It was a laborious life, full of distasteful and repugnant duties. We can readily imagine, with the aid of the striking picture which Fabre has drawn for us, what life was in these surroundings, and what the teaching was : " Between four high walls I see the court, a sort of bear-pit where the scholars quarrelled for the space beneath the boughs of a plane-tree; all around opened the class-rooms, oozing with damp and melancholy, like so many wild beasts' cages, deficient in light and air . . . for seats, a plank fixed to

the wall . . . in the middle a chair, the rushes
of the seat departed, a blackboard, and a stick
of chalk." [1]

Let the teachers of our spacious and well-
lighted schools of to-day ponder on these not so
distant years, and measure the progress accomplished. Evoking the memory of their humble
colleague of Carpentras, may they feel the true
greatness of his example : a noble and a glorious
example, of which they may well be proud.

And what pupils ! " Dirty, unmannerly : fifty
young scoundrels, children or big lads, with
whom," no doubt, " he used to squabble," but
whom, after all, he contrived to manage, and
by whom he was listened to and respected : for
he knew precisely what to say to them, and
how, while talking lightly, to teach them the most
serious things. For the joy of teaching, and
of continually learning by teaching others, made
everything endurable. Not only did he teach
them to read, write, and cipher, which then
included almost the entire programme of
primary education ; he endeavoured also to
place his own knowledge at their service, as he
himself acquired it.

It was not only his love of the work that sustained him ; it was the desire to escape from

the rut, to accomplish yet another stage ; to
emerge, in short, from so unsatisfactory a
position. Now nothing but physical and mathe-
matical science would allow him to entertain the
hope of " making an opening " in the world of
secondary schoolmasters. He accordingly began
to study physics, quite alone, " with an impossible
laboratory, experimenting after his own fashion " ;
and it was by teaching them to his pupils that he
learned first of all chemistry, inexpensively performing little elementary experiments before
them, " with pipe-bowls for crucibles and aniseed
flasks for retorts," and finally algebra, of which
he knew not a word before he gave his first
lesson.[2]

How he studied, what was the secret of his
method, he told his brother a few years later,
when the latter, marking time behind him, was
pursuing the same career. A very disappointing
career, no doubt, and far from lucrative, but
" one of the noblest ; one of those best fitted
for a noble spirit, and a lover of the good." [3]

Listen to the lesson which he gives his
brother :

" To-day is Thursday ; nothing calls you out
of doors ; you choose a thoroughly quiet retreat,
where the light is not too strong. There you
are, elbows on table, your thumbs to your ears,

and a book in front of you. The intelligence awakes ; the will holds the reins of it ; the outer world disappears, the ear no longer hears, the eye no longer sees, the body no longer exists ; the mind schools itself, recollects itself ; it is finding knowledge, and its insight increases. Then the hours pass quickly, quickly ; time has no measure. Now it is evening. What a day, great God ! But hosts of truths are grouped in the memory ; the difficulties which checked you yesterday have fused in the fire of reflection ; volumes have been devoured, and you are content with your day. . . .

" When something embarrasses you do not abuse the help of your colleagues ; with assistance the difficulty is only evaded ; with patience and reflection *it is overthrown*. Moreover, one knows thoroughly only what one learns oneself ; and I advise you earnestly, as far as possible, to have recourse to no aid other than reflection, above all for the sciences. A book of science is an enigma to be deciphered ; if some one gives you the key of the enigma nothing appears more simple and more natural than the explanation, but if a second enigma presents itself you will be as unskilful as you were with the first. . . .

" It is probable that you will get the chance of a few lessons ; do not by preference accept the easier and more lucrative, but rather the more difficult, even when the subject is one of which as yet you know nothing. The self-esteem which will not allow one's true character to be seen is a powerful aid to the will. Do not forget the method of Jules Janin, running from house to house in Paris for a few wretched lessons in Latin : ' Unable to get anything out of my stupid pupils, with the besotted son of the marquis I was simultaneously pupil and professor : I explained the ancient authors to myself, and so, in a few months, I went through an excellent course of rhetoric. . . .'

" Above all you must not be discouraged ; time is nothing provided the will is always alert, always active, and never distracted ; ' strength will come as you travel.'

" Try only for a few days this method of working, in which the whole energy, concentrated on one point, explodes like a mine and shatters obstacles ; try for a few days the force of patience, strength, and perseverance ; and you will see that nothing is impossible ! " 4

These serious reflections show very clearly that his mind was already as mature, as earnest, and as concentrated as it was ever to be.

Not only did he join example to precept ; he looked about him and began to observe nature in her own house. The doings of the mason bee, which he encountered for the first time, aroused his interest to such a pitch that, being no longer able to constrain his curiosity, he bought —at the cost of what privations !—Blanchard's *Natural History of the Articulata,* then a classic work, which he was to re-read a hundred times, and which he still retains, giving it the first place in his modest library, in memory of his early joys and emotions.

The rocks also arrested and captivated his attention : and already the first volumes were corpulent of what was eventually to become his gigantic herbiary. His brother, about to leave for Vezins on vacation, was told of the specimens which he wanted to complete his collection ; for although he had never set foot there since his first departure, he recalled, with remarkable pre-cision, all the plants that grew in his native countryside ; their haunts, their singularities, and the characteristics by which one could not fail to recognize them : as well as all the places which they chose by preference, where he used to wander as an urchin ; the *Parnassia palustris,* " which springs up in the damp meadows, below the beech-wood to the west of the village; which bears a superb white flower at the top of a slightly twisted stem, having an oval leaf about its middle "; the purple digitalis, " whose long spindles of great red flowers, speckled with white inside, and shaped like the fingers of a glove," border a certain road; all the ferns that grow on the wastes, " amid which it is often no easy task to recollect one's whereabouts," and on the arid hills all the heathers, pink, white, and bluish, with different foliage, " of which the innumerable species do not, however, very greatly differ." Nothing is to be neglected; " every plant, whatever it may be, great or little, rare or common, were it only a frond of moss, may have its interest." 5

Never weary of work, he accumulated all these treasures in his little museum, in order to study them the better; he collected all the coins exhumed from this ancient soil, formerly Roman, " records of humanity more eloquent than books," and which revealed to him the only method of learning and actually re-living history: for he saw in knowledge not merely a means of gaining his bread, but " something nobler; the means of raising the spirit in the contemplation of the truth, of isolating it at will from the miseries of reality, so to find, in these intellectual regions, the only hours of happiness that we may be permitted to taste." 6

Fabre was so steeped in this passion for knowledge that he wished to evoke it in his brother, now teacher at Lapalud, on the Rhône, not far from Orange. It seemed to him that he would delight in his wealth still better could he share it with another.7   He stimulated him, pricked him on, and sought to encourage the remarkable aptitude for mathematics with which he believed him endowed.   He employed his whole strength in breathing into the other's mind " that taste for the true and the beautiful " which possessed his own nature ;   he wished to share with him those stores of learning " which he had for some years so painfully amassed " ;   he would profit by the vacation to place them at his disposal ;   they would work together " and the light would come."   Above all his brother must not allow his intelligence to slumber, must beware of " extinguishing that divine light without which one can, it is true, attend to one's business, but which alone can make a man honourable and respected."

Let him, on the contrary, cultivate his mind incessantly, " the only patrimony on which either of us can count " ;   the reward would be his moral well-being, and, he hoped, his physical welfare also.

Once more he reinforced his advice by that excellent counsel which was always his own lodestar :

" Science, Frédéric, knowledge is everything. . . . You are too good a thinker not to say with me that no one can better employ his time than by acquiring fresh knowledge. . . . Work, then, when you have the opportunity . . . an opportunity that very few may possess, and for which you ought to be only too thankful. But I will stop, for I feel my enthusiasm is going to my head, and my reasons are so good already that I have no need of still more triumphant reasons to convince you." [8]

He had only one passion : shooting ; more especially the shooting of larks. This sport delighted him, " with the mirror darting its intermittent beams under the rays of the morning sun amid the general scintillation of the dewdrops and crystals of hoarfrost hanging on every blade of grass." [9]

His sight was admirably sure, and he rarely missed his aim. His passion for shooting was always sustained by the same motive : the desire to acquire fresh knowledge ; to examine unknown creatures close at hand; to discover what they ate and how they lived.

Later, when he again took up his gun, it was still because of his love of life : it was to enable him to enumerate, inventory, and interrogate his new compatriots, his feathered fellow-citizens of Sérignan; to inform himself of their diet, to reveal the contents of their crops and gizzards.

At one time he suddenly ceased to employ this distraction; he seems to have sacrificed it easily, under the stress of present necessities and cruel anxieties as to his uncertain future. "When we do not know where we shall be to-morrow nothing can distract us." [10]

His responsibilities were increasing. He had lately married. On the 30th October, 1844, he was wedded to a young girl of Carpentras, Marie Villard, and already a child was born. His parents, always unlucky, met nowhere with any success. By dint of many wanderings they had finally become stranded at Pierrelatte, the chief town of the canton of La Drôme, sheltered by the great rock which has given the place its name; and there again, of course, they kept a café, situated on the Place d'Armes.

The whole family was now assembled in the same district, a few miles only one from another : but Henri was really its head. Having heard that a quarrel had arisen between his brother and his mother, he wrote to Frédéric in reprimand; gently scolding him and begging him to set matters right, " even if all the wrongs were not on his side."

" My father, in one of his letters, complains that in spite of your nearness you have not yet been to see them. I know very well there is some reason for sulking; but what matter? Give it up: forget everything; do your best to put an end to all these petty and ugly estrangements. You will do so, won't you? I count on it, for the happiness of all." [11]

He was their arbitrator, their adviser, their oracle, their bond of union.

With all this, he was ready to attempt the two examinations which were to decide his future. Very shortly, at Montpellier, he passed almost successively, at an interval of only a few months the examinations for both his *baccalauréats;* and then the two licentiate examinations in mathematics and physical science.

While he was ardently studying for these examinations, sorrow for the first time knocked at his door. His first-born fell suddenly ill, and in a few days died. On this occasion all his ardent spirituality asserted itself, though in

stricken accents, in the letter which he wrote to
his brother to announce his loss :

" After a few days of a marked improvement,
which made me think he was saved, two large
teeth were cut . . . and in three days a dreadful fever took him, not from us, who will follow
him, but from this miserable world. Ah, poor
child, I shall always see you as you were during
those last moments, turning those wide, wandering eyes toward heaven, seeking the way to
your new country. With a heart full of tears,
I shall often let my thoughts go straying after
you ; but alas ! with the eyes of the body I
shall never see you again. I shall see you no
more : yet only a few days ago I was making
the finest plans for you. I used to work for
you only ; in my studies I thought only of you.
Grow up, I used to say, and I will pour into
your mind all the knowledge which has cost
me so dear, which I am hoarding little by little.
. . . But reflection leads me to higher thoughts.
I choke back the tears in my heart, and I con-
gratulate him that Heaven has mercifully spared
him this life of trials. . . . My poor child . . .
you will never, like your father, have to struggle
against poverty and misfortune ; you will never
know the bitterness of life, and the difficulties of
creating a position at a time when there are so

many paths that lead to failure . . . I weep
for you because we have lost you, but I rejoice
because you are happy. . . . You are happy,
and this is not the mad hope of a father broken
by sorrow; no, your last glance told me so,
too eloquently for me to doubt it. Oh, how
beautiful you were in your mortal pallor; the
last sigh on your lips, your gaze upon heaven,
and your soul ready to fly into the bosom of God !
Your last day was the most beautiful ! " [12]

Although study was his refuge, although he
was thereby able to live through these evil days
without too greatly feeling their weight, his
position was hateful, and he lived a wretched
life " from one day to another, like a beggar."

In those troublous times, when education was
of no account, it often happened that his teacher's
salary was several months in arrears, and the
city of Carpentras, " not being in funds," paid
it only by instalments, and even so kept him a
long time waiting. " One has to besiege the
paymaster's door merely to obtain a trifle on
account. I am ashamed of the whole business,
and I would gladly abandon my claim if I knew
where to raise any money." [13]

The genius of Balzac has recorded some unforgettable types of those poor and notable lives, at once so humble and so lofty. He has described the village curé and the country doctor. But how we should have loved to encounter in his gallery, among so many living portraits, a picture of the university life of fifty years ago ; and above all a picture of the small schoolmaster of other days, living a life so narrow, so slavish, so painful, and yet so full of worth, so imbued with the sense of duty, and withal so resigned ; a portrait for which Fabre might have served as model and prototype, and for which he himself has drawn an unforgettable sketch.

He awaited impatiently the news of his removal, very modestly limiting his ambitions to the hope of entering some *lycée* as professor of the sciences. His rector was not unnaturally astonished that a young man of such unusual worth, already twice a licentiate, should be so little appreciated by those in high places and allowed to stagnate so long in an inferior post, and one unworthy of him.

In the end, however, after much patient waiting, he became indignant ; as always, he could see nothing ahead. The chair of mathematics at Tournon escaped him. Another position, at Avignon, also " slipped through his fingers " ; why

or how he never knew. He " began to see clearly
what life is, and how difficult it is to make one's
mark amid all this army of schemers, beggars
and imbeciles who besiege every vacant post."

But his heart was " none the less hot with indignation " ; he had had enough of " Carpentras, that accursed little hole " ; and when the
vacations came round once more he " plainly
considered the question " and declared " that he
would never again set foot inside a communal
school." [14]

He wrote to the rector : " If instead of crush-
ing me into the narrow round of a primary school
they would give me some employment of the
kind for which my studies and ideas fit me, they
would know then what is hatching in my head
and what untirable activity there is in me." [15]

He resigned himself nevertheless ; he cursed
and swore and stormed at his fate ; but he had
once more to put up with it " for want of a
better." All the same " the injustice was too
unheard-of, and no one had ever seen or would
ever see the like : to give him two licentiate's
diplomas, and to make him conjugate verbs for
a pack of brats ! It was too much ! " [16]

III

CORSICA

At last the chair of physics fell vacant at the college of Ajaccio, the salary being £72, and he left for Corsica. His stay there was well calculated to impress him. There the intense impressionability which the little peasant of Aveyron received at birth could only be confirmed and increased. He felt that this superb and luxuriant nature was made for him, and that he was born for it; to understand and interpret it. He would lose himself in a delicious intoxication, amid the deep woodlands, the mountains rich with scented flowers, wandering through the *maquis,* the myrtle scrub, through jungles of lentisk and arbutus; barely containing his emotion when he passed beneath the great secular chestnut-trees of Bastelica, with their enormous trunks and leafy boughs, whose sombre majesty inspired in him a sort of melancholy at once poetic and religious. Before the

sea, with its infinite distances, he lingered in
ecstasy, listening to the song of the waves, and
gathering the marvellous shells which the snow-
white breakers left upon the beach, and whose
unfamiliar forms filled him with delight.

He was soon so accustomed to his new life in
peaceful Ajaccio, whose surroundings, decked in
eternal verdure, are so captivating and so beautiful, that in spite of a vague desire for change
he now dreaded to leave it. He never wearied
of admiring and exalting the beautiful and
majestic aspects of his new home. How he
longed to share his enthusiasm with his father
or his brother, as he rambled through the neighbouring *maquis!*

" The infinite, glittering sea at my feet, the
dreadful masses of granite overhead, the white,
dainty town seated beside the water, the endless
jungles of myrtle, which yield intoxicating perfumes, the wastes of brushwood which the
ploughshare has never turned, which cover the
mountains from base to summit; the fishing-
boats that plough the gulf: all this forms a
prospect so magnificent, so striking, that whosoever has beheld it must always long to see it
again." [1]

" What is their rock of Pierrelatte, that enor-

mous block of stone which overhangs the place
where they dwell, a reef which rises from the
surface of the ancient sea of alluvium, compared
with these blocks of uprooted granite which lie
upon the hillsides here? "

And what were the Aubrac hills which tra-
versed his native country; what was the Ventoux
even, that famous Alp, " beside the peaks which
rise about the gulf of Ajaccio, always crowned
with clouds and whitened with snow, even when
the soil of the plains is scorching and rings like
a fired brick? "

Time did nothing to abate these first impressions, and after more than a year on the island
he was still full of wonder " at the sight of these
granite crests, corroded by the severities of the
climate, jagged, overthrown by the lightning,
shattered by the slow but sure action of the
snows, and these vertiginous gulfs through which
the four winds of heaven go roaring; these vast
inclined planes on which snow-drifts form thirty,
sixty, and ninety feet in depth, and across which
flow winding watercourses which go to fill, drop
by drop, the yawning craters, there to form lakes,
black as ink when seen in the shadow, but blue
as heaven in the light. . . .

" But it would be impossible for me to give

you the least idea of this dizzy spectacle, this chaos of rocks, heaped in frightful disorder. When, closing my eyes, I contemplate these results of the convulsion of the soil in my mind's eye, when I hear the screaming of the eagles, which go wheeling through the bottomless abysses, whose inky shadows the eye dares hardly plumb, vertigo seizes me, and I open my eyes to reassure myself by the reality."

And he sends with his letter a few leaves of the snow immortelle—the *edelweiss*—plucked on the highest summits, amid the eternal snows; "you will put this in some book, and when, as you turn the leaves, the immortelle meets your eyes, it will give you an excuse for dreaming of the beautiful horrors of its native place." [2]

What a misfortune for him, what regret he would feel, "if he had now to go to some trivial country of plains, where he would die of boredom!"

For him everything was unfamiliar: not only the flora, but the maritime wealth of this singular country. He would set out of a morning, visiting the coves and creeks, roving along the beaches of this magnificent gulf, a lump of bread in his pocket, quenching his thirst with sea-water in default of fresh!

They were mornings full of rosy illusions, whose smiling hopes were revealed in his admirable letters to his brother. Already he meditated a conchology of Corsica, a colossal history of all the molluscs which live upon its soil or in its waters.3 He collected all the shells he could procure. He analysed, described, classed, and co-ordinated not only the marine species, but the terrestrial and freshwater shells also, extant or fossil. He asked his brother to collect for him all the shells he could find in the marshes of Lapalud, in the brooks and ditches of the neighbourhood of Orange. In his enthusiasm he tried to convince him of the immense interest of these researches, which might perhaps seem ridiculous or futile to him ; but let him only think of geology ; the humblest shell picked up might throw a sudden light upon the formation of this or that stratum. None are to be disdained : for men have considered, with reason, that they were honouring the memory of their eminent fellows by giving their names to the rarest and most beautiful. Witness the magnificent Helix dedicated to Raspail, which is found only in the caverns where the strawberry-tree grows amid the high mountains of Corsica.4

Moreover, he said, " the infinitesimal calculus of Leibnitz will show you that the architecture

of the Louvre is less learned than that of a
snail : the eternal geometer has unrolled his
transcendent spirals on the shell of the mollusc
that you, like the vulgar profane, know only
seasoned with spinach and Dutch cheese." [5]

For all that, he did not neglect his mathematics, in which, on the contrary, he found abundant and suggestive recreation. The properties
of a figure or a curve which he had newly
discovered prevented his sleep for several
nights.

" All this morning I have been busy with
star-shaped polygons, and have proceeded from
surprise to surprise . . . perceiving in the distance, as I advanced, unforeseen and marvellous
consequences."

Here, among others, is one question which
suddenly presented itself to his mind " in the
midst of the spikes " of his polygons : what
would be the period of the rotation of the sun
on its own centre if its atmosphere reached as
far as the earth? And this question gave rise
to another, " without which the sequence stops
then and there ; number, space, movement, and
order form a single chain, the first link of which
sets all the rest in motion." [6] And the hours
went by quickly, so quickly with x, the plants

and the shells, that "literally there was no time to eat."

For Fabre was born a poet, and mathematics borders upon poetry; he saw in algebra "the most magnificent flights," and the figures of analytical geometry unrolled themselves in his imagination "in superb strophes"; the Ellipse, "the trajectory of the planets, with its two related foci, sending from one to the other a constant sum of vector radii"; the Hyperbole, "with repulsive foci, the desperate curve which plunges into space in infinite tentacles, approaching closer and closer to a straight line, the asymptote, without ever finally attaining it"; the Parabola, "which seeks fruitlessly in the infinite for its second, lost centre: it is the trajectory of the bomb: it is the path of certain comets which come one day to visit our sun, then flee into the depths whence they never return." [7]

And one fine morning we behold him mounting, thrilled by a lyric passion, to the lofty regions in which Number, "irresistible, omnipotent, keystone of the vault of the universe, rules at once Time and Space." He ascends, he rushes forward, farther than the chariot—

"Beyond the Husbandman who ploughs in space
And sows the suns in furrows of the skies."

He ascends those tracks of flame, where on high

"in those lists inane
Wise regulator, Number holds the reins
  Of those indomitable steeds;
Number has set a bit i' the foaming mouths
Of these Leviathans, and with nervous hand
  Controls them in their tracks;

Their smoking flanks beneath the yoke in vain
Quiver; their nostrils vainly void as foam
Dense tides of lava; and in vain they rear;
For Number on their mettled haunches poised
Holds them, or duly with the rein controls,
Or in their flanks buries his spur divine." [8]

Later he confessed all that he owed, as a writer, to geometry, whose severe discipline forms and exercises the mind, gives it the salutary habit of precision and lucidity, and puts it on its guard against terms which are incorrect or unduly vague, giving it qualities far superior to all the " tropes of rhetoric."

It was then that he became the pupil of Requien of Avignon, the retired botanist, a lofty but somewhat limited mind, who was hardly capable of opening up other horizons to him. But Requien did at least enrich his memory by a prodigious quantity of names of plants with which he had not been acquainted. He revealed

to him the immense flora of Corsica, which he
himself had come to study, and for which Fabre
was to gather such a vast amount of material.

Fabre found in Requien more especially a
friend " proof against anything " ; and when the
latter died almost suddenly at Bonifacio, Fabre
was overwhelmed by the sad news. On that
very day he had on the table before him a parcel
of plants gathered for the dead botanist. " I
cannot let my eyes rest upon it," he wrote at
the time, " without feeling my heart wrung and
my sight dim with tears." 9

But the most admirably fruitful encounter, as
it exercised the profoundest influence upon his
destiny, was his meeting with Moquin-Tandon,
a Toulouse professor who followed Requien to
Corsica, to complete the work which the latter
had left unfinished : the complete inventory of
the prodigious wealth of vegetation, of the innumerable species and varieties which Fabre and
he collected together, on the slopes and summits of Monte Renoso, often botanizing " up
in the clouds, mantle on back and numb with
cold." 10

Moquin-Tandon was not merely a skilful
naturalist ; he was one of the most eloquent and
scholarly scientists of his time. Fabre owed

to him, not his genius, to be sure, but the definite
indication of the path he was finally to take, and
from which he was never again to stray.

Moquin-Tandon, a brilliant writer and " an
ingenious poet in his Montpellerian [11] dialect,"
taught Fabre never to forget the value of style
and the importance of form, even in the exposition of a purely descriptive science such as
botany. He did even more, by one day suddenly showing Fabre, between the fruit and the
cheese, " in a plate of water," the anatomy of
the snail. This was his first introduction to his
true destiny before the final revelation of which
I shall presently speak. Fabre understood then
and there that he could do decidedly better than
to stick to mathematics, though his whole career
would feel the effects of that study.

" Geometers are made ; naturalists are born
ready-made," he wrote to his brother, still excited
by this incident, " and you know better than any
one whether natural history is not my favourite
science." [12]

From that time forward he began to collect
not only dead, inert, or dessicated forms, mere
material for study, with the aim of satisfying his
curiosity ; he began to dissect with ardour, a
thing he had never done before. He housed
his tiny guests in his cupboard ; and occupied

himself, as he was always to do in the future, with the smaller living creatures only.

" I am dissecting the infinitely little ; my scalpels are tiny daggers which I make myself out of fine needles ; my marble slab is the bottom of a saucer ; my prisoners are lodged by the dozen in old match-boxes ; *maxime miranda in minimis*." [13]

Roaming at night along the marshy beaches, he contracted fever, and several terrible attacks, accompanied by alarming tremors, left him so bloodless and feeble that, much against his will, he had to beg for relief, and even insist upon his prompt return to the mainland. In the meantime he obtained sick-leave, and returned to Provence after a terrible crossing which lasted no less than three days and two nights, on a sea so furious that he gave himself up for lost. [14]

Slowly he recovered his health, and after a second but brief stay at Ajaccio he received the news of his appointment to the *lycée* of Avignon.[15]

He returned with his imagination enriched and his mind expanded, with settled ideas, and thoroughly ripe for his task.

IV

AT AVIGNON

THE resolute worker resumed his indefatigable labours with an ardour greater than ever, for now he was haunted by a noble ambition, that of becoming a teacher of the superior grade, and of " talking plants and animals " in a chair of the faculty. With this end in view he added to his two diplomas—those of mathematics and physics—a third certificate, that of natural sciences. His success was triumphant.

Already tenacious and fearless in affirming what he believed to be the truth, he astonished and bewildered the professors of Toulouse. Among the subjects touched upon by the examiners was the famous question of spontaneous generation, which was then so vital, and which gave rise to so many impassioned discussions. The examiner, as it chanced, was one of the leading apostles of this doctrine. The future adversary of Darwin, at the risk of failure, did not scruple to argue with him, and to put forward his personal convictions and his own arguments. He decided the vexed question in his own way, on his own responsibility. A personality already so striking was regarded with admiration; a candidate so far out of the ordinary was welcomed with enthusiasm, and but for the insufficiency of the budget which so scantily met the needs of public instruction his examination fees would have been returned.[1]

Why, after this brilliant success, was Fabre not tempted to enter himself for a fellowship, which would later in his career have averted so many disappointments? It was doubtless because he felt, obscurely, that his ideal future lay along other lines, and that he would have been taking a wrong turning. Despite all the solicitations which were addressed to him he would think of nothing but " his beloved studies in natural history ";[2] he feared to lose precious time in preparing himself for a competitive examination; " to compromise by such labour, which he felt would be fruitless,"[3] the studies which he had already commenced, and the inquiries already carried out in Corsica. He was busy with his first original labours, the theses which he was preparing with a view to his doctorate in natural science, " which might one day open the doors of a faculty for him, far more easily than would a fellowship and its mathematics." 4

At heart he was utterly careless of dignities and degrees. He worked only to learn, not to attain and follow up a settled calling. What he hoped above all was to succeed in devoting all his leisure to those marvellous natural sciences in which he could vaguely foresee studies full of interest ; something animated and vital ; a thousand fascinating themes, and an atmosphere of poetry.

His genius, as yet invisible, was ripening in obscurity, but was ready to come forth ; he lacked only the propitious circumstance which would allow him to unfold his wings.

He was seeking them in vain when a volume by Léon Dufour, the famous entomologist, who then lived in the depths of the Landes, fell by chance into his hands, and lit the first spark of that beacon which was presently to decide the definite trend of his ideas.

It was this incident which then and there developed the germs already latent within him. These had only awaited such an occasion as that which so fortunately came to pass one evening of the winter of 1854.

Fabre offers yet another example of the part so often played by chance in the manifestations of talent. How many have suddenly felt the unexpected awakening of gifts which they did not suspect, as a result of some unusual circumstance !

Was it not simply as a result of having read a note by the Russian chemist Mitscherlich on the comparison of the specific characteristics of certain crystals that Pasteur so enthusiastically took up his researches into molecular asymmetry which were the starting-point of so many wonderful discoveries?

Again, we need only recall the case of Brother Huber, the celebrated observer of the bee, who, having out of simple curiosity undertaken to verify certain experiments of Réaumur's, was so completely and immediately fascinated by the subject that it became the object of the rest of his life.

Again, we may ask what Claude Bernard would have been had he not met Magendie? Similarly Léon Dufour's little work was to Fabre the road to Damascus, the electric impulse which decided his vocation.

It dealt with a very singular fact concerning

the manners of one of the hymenoptera, a wasp, a Cerceris, in whose nest Dufour had found small coleoptera of the genus Buprestis, which, under all the appearances of death, retained intact for an incredible time their sumptuous costume, gleaming with gold, copper, and emerald, while the tissues remained perfectly fresh. In a word, the victims of Cerceris, far from being desiccated or putrefied, were found in a state of integrity which was altogether paradoxical.

Dufour merely believed that the Buprestes were dead, and he gave an attempted explanation of the phenomenon.

Fabre, his curiosity and interest aroused, wished to observe the facts for himself; and, to his great surprise, he discovered how incomplete and insufficiently verified were the observations of the man who was at that time known as " the patriarch of entomologists."

From that moment he saw his way ahead; he suspected that there was still much to discover and much to revise in this vast department of nature, and conceived the idea of resuming the work so splendidly outlined by Réaumur and the two Hubers, but almost completely neglected since the days of those illustrious masters. He divined that here were fresh pastures, a vast unexplored country to be opened up, an entire unimagined science to be founded, wonderful secrets to be discovered, magnificent problems to be solved, and he dreamed of consecrating himself unreservedly, of employing his whole life in the pursuit of this object ; that long life whose fruitful activity was to extend over nearly ninety years, and which was to be so " representative " by the dignity of the man, the probity of the expert, the genius of the observer, and the originality of the writer.

The year 1855 saw the first appearance, in the *Annales des sciences naturelles,* of the famous memoir which marked the beginning of his fame : the history, which might well be called marvellous and incredible, of the great Cerceris, a giant wasp and " the finest of the Hymenoptera which hunt for booty at the foot of Mont Ventoux." [5]

Fabre was now thirty-two years old, and his situation as assistant-professor of physics was somewhat precarious. From the £72 which he drew at Ajaccio, an overseas post, his salary was reduced, on his return to the mainland, to £64, and during the whole of his stay at Avignon he obtained neither promotion nor the smallest increase of pay, excepting a few additional profits which were unconnected with his habitual

duties. When he left the university after twenty
well-filled years, he left as he had entered, with
the same title, rank, and salary of a mere assistant-professor.

Yet all about him "everywhere and for every
one, all was black indeed": his family had increased and therewith his expenses; there were
now seven at table every day. Very shortly his
modest salary would no longer suffice; he was
obliged to supplement it by all sorts of hack-
work—classes, "repetitions," private lessons;
tasks which repelled him, for they absorbed all
his available time; they prevented him from
giving himself up to his favourite studies, to
his silent and solitary observations. Nevertheless, he acquitted himself of these duties
patiently and conscientiously, for at heart he
loved his profession, and was rather a fellow-
disciple than a master to his pupils. For this
reason all those about him worked with praise-
worthy assiduity; even the worst elements, the
black sheep, the "bad eggs" of other classes,
with him were suddenly transformed and as
attentive as the rest. Although he knew how to
keep order, how to make himself respected, and
could on occasion deal severely and speak
sternly, so that very few dared to forget them-

selves before him, he knew also how to be merry
with his pupils, chatting with them familiarly,
putting himself in their place, entering into their
ideas, and making himself their rival. If life was
laborious under his *ferula,* it was also merry.
The best proof of this is the fact that of all his
colleagues at the *lycée* he was the only one who
had no nickname, a rarity in scholastic annals.

He did not therefore object to these lessons ;
but while at Carpentras he was made much of
and praised by the principal, was a general
favourite, and had perfect liberty to follow his
inspiration during his partly gratuitous classes,
here the hours and the programme tied him
down, which was precisely what he found
insupportable.

Everything made things difficult for him here :
his external self ; his character, ever so little shy
and unsocial ; his temperament, which was made
for solitude.

In the thick of this hierarchical society of
university professors he remained independent ;
he knew nothing of what was said or what was
happening in the college, and his colleagues
were always better informed than he.[6] As he
was not a fellow, he was made to feel the fact
and was treated as a subordinate ; the others,

who prided themselves on the title, and who
were incapable of recognizing his merit, which
was a little beyond them, were jealous of him, all
the more inasmuch as his name was momentarily
noised abroad, and they revenged themselves by
calling him " the fly " among themselves, by way
of allusion to his favourite subject.[7]

Indifferent to distinctions, as well as to those
who bore them, contemptuous of etiquette, and
incapable of putting constraint upon his nature,
he remained an " outsider," and refused to
comply with a host of factitious or worldly obligations which he regarded as useless or dis-
gusting. Thus even at Ajaccio he managed to
escape the customary ceremonies of New Year's
Day.

" Good society I avoid as much as possible;
I prefer my own company. So I have seen no
one; I did not respond to the principal's invitation to make the official round of visits." [8]

When obliged to accept some invitation, apart
from occasions of too great solemnity, when he
was really constrained to dress himself in the
complete livery of circumstance and ceremony,
he remained faithful to his black felt hat, which
made a blot among all the carefully polished
" toppers " of his colleagues. He was called to

order; he was reprimanded; he obeyed un-
willingly, or worse, he resisted; he revolted,
and threatened to send in his resignation. To
pay court to people, to endeavour to make himself pleasant, to grovel before a superior, were
to him impossibilities. He could neither solicit,
nor sail with the wind, nor force himself on
others, nor even make use of his relations.

However, when he went to Paris to take his
doctor's degree in natural sciences, he did not
forget Moquin-Tandon, who had formerly, in
Corsica, revealed to him the nature of biology,
and whom he himself had received and entertained in his humble home.

The ex-professor of Toulouse, who was now
eminent in his speciality, occupied the chair of
natural history in the faculty of medicine in
Paris. What better occasion could he wish of
introducing himself to a highly placed official?
Fabre had formerly been his host; he could
recall the happy hours they had spent together;
he could explain his plans, and ask for the professor's assistance! Fate pointed to him as a
protector. But if Fabre had been capable of
climbing the professor's stairs with some such
ambitious desires, he would quickly have been
disabused.

The " dear master " had long ago forgotten the little professor of Ajaccio, and his welcome was by no means such as Fabre had the right to expect. Far from insisting, he was disheartened, perhaps a little humiliated, and hastened to take his leave.

The theses which Fabre brought with him, and which, he had thought, ought to lead him one day to a university professorship, did not, as a matter of fact, contain anything very essentially original.

He had been attracted, indeed fascinated, by all the singularities presented by the strange family of the orchids ; the asymmetry of their blossoms, the unusual structure of their pollen, and their innumerable seeds ; but as for the curious rounded and duplicated tubercles which many of them bore at their base, what precisely were they? The greatest botanists—de Candolle, A. de Jussieu—had perceived in them nothing more than roots. Fabre demonstrated in his thesis that these singular organs are in reality merely buds, true branches or shoots, modified and disguised, analogous to the metamorphosed tubercle of the potato.[9]

He added also a curious memoir on the phosphorescence of the agaric of the olive-tree, a phenomenon to which he was to return at a later date.

In the field of zoology his scalpel revealed the complicated structure of the reproductive organs of the Centipedes (Millepedes), hitherto so confused and misunderstood; as also certain peculiarities of the development of these curious creatures, so interesting from the point of view of the zoological philosopher,[10] for he had become expert in handling not only the magnifying glass, which was always with him, but also the microscope, which discovers so many infinite wonders in the lowest creatures, yet which was not of particular service in any of the beautiful observations upon which his fame is built.

Returning to Avignon, in the possession of his new degree, he commenced an important task which took him nearly twenty years to complete : a painstaking treatise on the Sphæriaceæ of Vaucluse, that singular family of fungi which cover fallen leaves and dead twigs with their blackish fructifications; a remarkable piece of work, full of the most valuable documentation, as were the theses whose subjects I have just detailed; but without belittling the fame of their author, one may say that another, in his place, might have acquitted himself as well.

Although he continued to undertake researches
of limited interest and importance, although he
persisted in dissecting plants, and, although he
disliked it, in " disembowelling animals," the fact
was that apart from Thursdays and Sundays it
was scarcely possible for him to escape from his
week's work; hardly possible to snatch sufficient
leisure to undertake the studies toward which he
felt himself more particularly drawn. Tied down
by his duties, which held him bound to a discipline that only left him brief moments, and
by the forced hack-work imposed upon him by
the necessity of earning his daily bread, he had
scarcely any time for observation excepting
vacations and holidays.

Then he would hasten to Carpentras, happy
to hold the key to the meadows, and wander
across country and along the sunken lanes, collecting his beautiful insects, breathing the free
air, the scent of the vines and olives, and gazing
upon Mont Ventoux, close at hand, whose silver
summit would now be hidden in the clouds and
now would glitter in the rays of the sun.

Carpentras was not merely the country in
which his wife's parents dwelt : it was, above all,
a unique and privileged home for insects; not
on account of its flora, but because of the soil,

a kind of limestone mingled with sand and clay, a soft marl, in which the burrowing hymenoptera could easily establish their burrows and their nests. Certain of them, indeed, lived only there, or at least it would have been extremely difficult to find them elsewhere ; such was the famous Cerceris ; such again, was the yellow-winged Sphex, that other wasp which so artistically stabs and paralyses the cricket, " the brown violinist of the clods."

At Carpentras too the Anthophoræ lived in abundance ; those wild bees with whom the vexed and enigmatic history of the Sitaris and the Meloë is bound up ; those little beetles, cousins of the Cantharides, whose complex metamorphoses and astonishing and peculiar habits have been revealed by Fabre. This memoir marked the second stage of his scientific career, and followed, at an interval of two years, the magnificent observations on the Cerceris.

These two studies, true masterpieces of science, already constituted two excellent titles to fame, and would by themselves have sufficed to fill a naturalist's whole lifetime and to make his name illustrious.

From that time forward he had no peer. The Institute awarded him one of its Montyon [11]

prizes, " an honour of which, needless to say, he
had never dreamed." [12] Darwin, in his celebrated work on the *Origin of Species,* which
appeared precisely at this moment, speaks of
Fabre somewhere as " the inimitable observer." [13]

Exploring the immediate surroundings of
Avignon, he very soon discovered fresh localities
frequented almost exclusively by other insects,
whose habits in their turn absorbed his whole
attention.

First of these was the sandy plateau of the
Angles, where every spring, in the sunlit pastures
so beloved of the sheep, the *Scarabæus sacer,*
with his incurved feet and clumsy legs, commences to roll his everlasting pellet, " to the
ancients the image of the world." His history,
since the time of the Pharaohs, had been nothing
but a tissue of legends ; but stripping it of the
embroidery of fiction, and referring it to the
facts of nature, Fabre demonstrated that the true
story is even more marvellous than all the tales
of ancient Egypt. He narrated its actual life,
the object of its task, and its comical and ex-
hilarating performances. But such is the
subtlety of these delicate and difficult researches
that nearly forty years were required to complete
the study of its habits and to solve the mystery
of its cradle. [14]

On the right bank of the Rhône, facing the embouchure of the Durance, is a small wood of oak-trees, the wood of Des Issarts. This again, for many reasons, was one of his favourite spots. There, " lying flat on the ground, his head in the shadow of some rabbit's burrow," or sheltered from the sun by a great umbrella, " while the blue-winged locusts frisked for joy," he would follow the rapid and sibilant flight of the elegant Bembex, carrying their daily ration of diptera to her larvæ, at the bottom of her burrow, deep in the fine sand." [15]

He did not always go thither alone : sometimes, on Sundays, he would take his pupils with him, to spend a morning in the fields, " at the ineffable festival of the awakening of life in the spring." [16]

Those most dear to him, those who in the subsequent years have remained the object of a special affection, were Devillario, Bordone, and Vayssières,[17] " young people with warm hearts and smiling imaginations, overflowing with that springtime sap of life which makes us so expansive and so eager to know.

Among them he was " the eldest, their master, but still more their companion and friend " ; lighting in them his own sacred fire, and amazing them by the deftness of his fingers and the acuteness of his lynx-like eyes. Furnished with a notebook and all the tools of the naturalist—lens, net, and little boxes of sawdust steeped in anæsthetic for the capture of rare specimens—they would wander "along the paths bordered with hawthorn and hyæbla, simple and childlike folk," probing the bushes, scratching up the sand, raising stones, running the net along hedge and meadow, with explosions of delight when they made some splendid capture or discovered some unrecorded marvel of the entomological world.

It was not only on the banks of the Rhône or the sandy plateau of Avignon that they sought adventure thus, "discussing things and other things," but as far as the slopes of Mont Ventoux, for which Fabre had always felt an inexplicable and invincible attraction, and whose ascent he accomplished more than twenty times, so that at last he knew all its secrets, all the gamut of its vegetation, the wealth of the varied flora which climb its flanks from base to summit, and which range "from the scarlet flowers of the pomegranate to the violet of Mont Cenis and the Alpine forget-me-not," [18] as well as the antediluvian fauna revealed amid its entrails, a vast ossuary rich in fossils.

His disciples, all of whom, without exception, regarded him with absolute worship, have retained the memory of his wit, his enthusiasm, his geniality and his infectious gaiety, and also of the singular uncertainty of his temperament; for on some days he would not speak a word from the beginning to the end of his walk.

Even his temper, ordinarily gentle and easy, would suddenly become hasty and violent, and would break out into terrible explosions when a sudden annoyance set him beside himself; for instance, when he was the butt of some ill-natured trick, or when, in spite of the lucidity of his explanations, he felt that he had not been properly understood. Perhaps he inherited this from his mother, a rebellious, crotchety, somewhat fantastic person, by whose temper he himself had suffered.

But the young people who surrounded him were far from being upset by these contrasts of temperament, in which they themselves saw nothing but natural annoyance, and the corollary, as it were, of his abounding vitality.[19]

It was because he was the only university teacher in Avignon to occupy himself with entomology that Pasteur visited him in 1865. The illustrious chemist had been striving to check

the plague that was devastating the silkworm
nurseries, and as he knew nothing of the subject
which he proposed to study, not even understanding the constitution of the cocoon or the evolution
of the silkworm, he sought out Fabre in order
to obtain from his store of entomological wisdom
the elementary ideas which he would find indispensable. Fabre has told us, in a moving page,[20]
with what a total lack of comprehension of
" poverty in a black coat " the great scientist
gazed at his poor home. Preoccupied by another
problem, that of the amelioration of wines by
means of heat, Pasteur asked him point-blank—
him, the humble proletarian of the university
caste, who drank only the cheapest wine of the
country—to show him his cellar. " My cellar !
Why not my vaults, my dusty bottles, labelled
according to age and vintage ! But Pasteur
insisted. Then, pointing with my finger, I
showed him, in a corner of the kitchen, a chair
with all the straw gone, and on this chair a two-
gallon demijohn : ' There is my cave, monsieur ! ' "

If the country professor was embarrassed by
the chilliness of the other, he was none the less
shocked by his attitude. It would seem, from
what Fabre has said, that Pasteur treated him
with a hauteur which was slightly disdainful. The
ignorant genius questioned his humble colleague,

distantly giving him his orders, explaining his
plans and his ideas, and informing him in what
directions he required assistance.

After this, we cannot be surprised if the
naturalist was silent. How could sympathetic
relations have survived this first meeting? Fabre
could not forgive it. His own character was
too independent to accommodate itself to
Pasteur's. Yet never, perhaps, were two men
made for a better understanding. They were
equally expert in exercising their admirable
powers of vision in the vast field of nature,
equally critical of self, equally careful never to
depart from the strict limits of the facts; and
they were, one may say, equally eminent in the
domain of invention, different though their for-
tunes may have been; for the sublimity of
scientific discoveries, however full of genius they
may be, is often measured only by the immediate
consequences drawn therefrom and the practical
importance of their results.

In reality, were they not two rivals, worthy
of being placed side by side in the paradise of
sages? Both of them, the one by demolishing
the theory of spontaneous generation, the other
by refuting the mechanical theory of the origin
of instincts, have brought into due prominence

the great unknown and mysterious forces which
seem destined to hold eternally in suspense the
profound enigma of life.

Now he was anxious not to leave the Vaucluse
district, the scene of his first success, and a place
so fruitful in subjects of study. He wished to
remain close to his insects, and also near the
precious library and the rich collections which
Requien had left by will to the town of Avignon.
In spite of the meagreness of his salary, he
asked for nothing more; and, what is more,
by an inconsequence which is by no means
incomprehensible, he avoided everything that
might have resulted in a more profitable position
elsewhere, and evaded all proposals of further
promotion. Twice, at Poitiers and Marseilles,
he refused a post as assistant professor, not
regarding the advantages sufficient to balance the
expenses of removal.[21]

It is true that his modest position was slightly
improved; at the *lycée* he had just been
appointed drawing-master, thanks to his knowledge of design, for he could draw—indeed, what
could he not do? The city, on the other hand,
appointed him conservator of the Requien
Museum, and presently municipal lecturer, so
that his earnings were increased by £48 per

annum, and he was at last able to abandon
" those abominable private lessons," [22] which the
insufficiency of his income had hitherto forced
him to accept. These new duties, which naturally
demanded much time and much labour, kept
him almost as badly tied as he had been before.

To be rich enough to set himself free ; to be
master of all his time, to be able to devote
himself entirely to his chosen work : this
was his dream, his constant preoccupation : it
haunted him ; it was a fixed idea.

Such was the principal motive of his inquiry
into the properties of madder, the colouring principle of which he succeeded in extracting directly,
by a perfectly simple method, which for a time
very advantageously replaced the extremely
primitive methods of the old dyers, who used
a simple extract of madder ; a crude preparation which necessitated long and expensive
manipulations.[23]

He had been working at this for eight years
when Victor Duruy, Minister of Public Instruction and Grand Master of the University, came
to surprise him in his laboratory at Saint-Martial,
in the full fever of research. Whatever was
Duruy's idea in entering into relations with him,
it seems that from their first meeting the two

men were really taken with one another : there
were, between them, so many close affinities of
taste and character. Duruy found in Fabre a
man of his own temper ; for his, like Fabre's,
was a modest and simple nature. Both came of
the people, and the principal motive of each was
the same ideal of work, emancipation, and
progress.

A little later Duruy summoned the modest
sage of Avignon to Paris, with particular
insistence ; he was full of attentions and of
forethought, and made him there and then a
chevalier of the Legion of Honour ; a distinction
of which Fabre was far from being proud, and
which he was careful never to obtrude ; but he
nevertheless always thought of it with a certain
tenderness, as a beloved " relic " in memory of
this illustrious friend.

On the following day the naturalist was con-
veyed to the Tuileries to be presented to the
Emperor. You must not suppose that he was
in the least disturbed at the idea of finding himself face to face with royalty. In the presence
of all these bedizened folk, in his coat of a cut
which was doubtless already superannuated, he
cared little for the impression he might produce.
As good an observer of men as of beasts, he

gazed quietly about him ; he exchanged a few
words with the Emperor, who was " quite
simple," almost suppressed, his eyes always
half-closed ; he watched the coming and going
of " the chamberlains with short breeches and
silver-buckled shoes, great scarabæi, clad with
café au lait wing-cases, moving with a formal
gait." Already he sighed regretfully ; he was
bored ; he was on the rack, and for nothing in
the world would he have repeated the experience.
He did not even feel the least desire to visit the
vaunted collections of the Museum. He longed
to return ; to find himself once more among his
dear insects ; to see his grey olive-trees, full
of the frolicsome cicadæ ; his wastes and commons, which smelt so sweet of thyme and
cypress ; above all, to return to his furnace and
retorts, in order to complete his discovery as
quickly as possible.

But others profited by his happy conceptions.
Like the cicada, the Cigale of his fable,* which
makes a " honeyed reek " flow from—

> " the bark
> Tender and juicy, of the bough,"

on which it is quickly supplanted by

> " Fly, drone, wasp, beetle too with hornèd head," [24]

---

* See *Social Life in the Insect World*, by J. H. Fabre
(The Century Co., 1912).

who

"Now lick their honey'd lips, and feed at leisure,"

so, after he had painfully laboured for twelve
years in his well, he saw others, more cunning
than he, come to his perch, who by dint of
"stamping on his toe," succeeded in ousting
him. Pending the appearance of artificial
alizarine, which was presently to turn the whole
madder industry upside down, these more
sophisticated persons were able to benefit at
leisure by the ingenious processes discovered by
Fabre, so that the practical result of so much
assiduity, so much patient research, was absolutely nil, and he found himself as poor as ever.

So faded his dream : and, if we except his
domestic griefs, this was certainly the deepest
and cruellest disappointment he had ever experienced.

Thenceforth he saw his salvation only in the
writing of textbooks, which were at last to throw
open the door of freedom. Already he had set
to work, under the powerful stimulus of Duruy,
preoccupied as he always was by his incessant
desire for freedom. The first rudiments of his
Agricultural Chemistry, which sounded so fresh
a note in the matter of teaching, had given
an instance and a measure of his capabilities.

But he did not seriously devote himself to this project until after the industrial failure and the distressing miscarriage of his madder process; and not until he had been previously assured of the co-operation of Charles Delagrave, a young publisher, whose fortunate intervention contributed in no small degree to his deliverance. Confident in his vast powers of work, and divining his incomparable talent as *popularizer*, Delagrave felt that he could promise Fabre that he would never leave him without work; and this promise was all the more comforting, in that the University, despite his twenty-eight years of assiduous service, would not accord him the smallest pension.

Victor Duruy was the great restorer of education in France, from elementary and primary education, which should date, from his great ministry, the era of its deliverance, to the secondary education which he himself created in every part. He was also the real initiator of secular instruction in France, and the Third Republic has done little but resume his work, develop his ideas, and extend his programme. Finally, by instituting classes for adults, the evening classes which enabled workmen, peasants, *bourgeois*, and young women to fill the gaps in their education, he gave reality to the generous and fruitful idea that it is possible for all to divide life into two parts, one having for its object our material needs and our daily bread, and the other consecrated to the spiritual life and the delights of the Ideal.

At the same time he emancipated the young women of France, formerly under the exclusive tutelage of the clergy, and opened to them for the first time the golden gates of knowledge ; an audacious innovation, and formidable withal, for it shrewdly touched the interests of the Church, struck a blow at her ever-increasing influence, and clashed with her consecrated privileges and age-long prejudices.[25]

At Avignon Fabre was instructed to give his personal services. He gave them with all his heart ; and it was then that he undertook, in the ancient Abbey of Saint-Martial, those famous free lectures which have remained celebrated in the memory of that generation. There, under the ancient Gothic vault, among the pupils of the primary Normal College, an eager crowd of listeners pressed to hear him ; and among the most assiduous was Roumanille, the friend of Mistral, he who so exquisitely wove into his harmonies " the laughter of young maidens and the flowers of springtime." No one expounded a fact better than Fabre; no one explained it so fully and so clearly. No one could teach as he did, in a fashion so simple, so animated, so picturesque, and by methods so original.

He was indeed convinced that even in early childhood it was possible for both boys and girls to learn and to love many subjects which had hitherto never been proposed; and in particular that Natural History which to him was a book in which all the world might read, but that university methods had reduced it to a tedious and useless study in which the letter " killed the life."

He knew the secret of communicating his conviction, his profound faith, to his hearers : that sacred fire which animated him, that passion for all the creatures of nature.

These lectures took place in the evening, twice a week, alternately with the municipal lectures, to which Fabre brought no less application and ardour. In the intention of those who instituted them these latter were above all to be practical and scientific, dealing with science applied to agriculture, the arts, and industry.

But might he not also expect auditors of another quality, in love only with the ideal, " who, without troubling about the possible applications of scientific theory, desired above all to be initiated into the action of the forces which rule nature, and thereby to open to their minds more wondrous horizons "?

Such were the noble scruples which troubled his conscience, and which appeared in the letter which he addressed to the administration of the city, when he was entrusted by the latter with what he regarded as a lofty and most important mission.

". . . Is it to be understood that every purely scientific aspect, incapable of immediate application, is to be rigorously banished from these lessons? Is it to be understood that, confined to an impassable circle, the value of every truth must be reckoned at so much per hundred, and that I must silently pass over all that aims only at satisfying a laudable desire of knowledge? No, gentlemen, for then these lectures would lack a very essential thing: the spirit which gives life ! " [26]

Physically, according to the testimony of his contemporaries, he was already as an admirable photograph represents him twenty years later: he wore a large black felt hat; his face was shaven, the chin strong and wilful, the eyes vigilant, deep-set and penetrating; he hardly changed, and it was thus I saw him later, at a more advanced age.

The ancient Abbey of Saint-Martial, where these lectures were given, was occupied also by the Requien Museum, of which Fabre had charge. It was here that he one day met John Stuart Mill.

The celebrated philosopher and economist had just lost his wife : " the most precious friend-ship of his life " [27] was ended. It was only after long waiting that he had been able to marry her. Subjected at an early age by a father devoid of tenderness and formidably severe to the harshest of disciplines, he had learned in childhood "what is usually learned only by a man." Scarcely out of his long clothes, he was construing Herodotus and the dialogues of Plato, and the whole of his dreary youth was spent in covering the vast field of the moral and mathe-matical sciences. His heart, always suppressed, never really expanded until he met Mrs. Harriett Taylor.

This was one of those privileged beings such as seem as a rule to exist only in poetry and literature ; a woman as beautiful as she was astonishingly gifted with the rarest faculties ; combining with the most searching intelligence

and the most persuasive eloquence so exquisite
a sensitiveness that she seemed often to divine
events in advance.

Mill possessed her at last for a few years
only, and he had resigned his post in the offices
of the East India Company to enjoy * a studious
retreat in the enchanted atmosphere of southern
Europe when suddenly at Avignon Harriett Mill
was carried off by a violent illness.

From that time the philosopher's horizon was
suddenly contracted to the limit of those places
whence had vanished the adored companion and
the beneficent genius who had been the sole
charm of his entire existence. Overwhelmed
with grief, he acquired a small country house
in one of the least frequented parts of the
suburbs of Avignon, close to the cemetery
where the beloved dead was laid to rest
for ever. A silent alley of planes and mul-
berry-trees led to the threshold, which was
shaded by the delicate foliage of a myrtle. All
about he had planted a dense hedge of hawthorn,
cypress, and arborvitæ, above which, from the
vantage of a small terrace, built, under his orders,
at the level of the first floor, he could see, day

* Mill retired in 1858, when the government of India
passed to the Crown. He had married Mrs. John Taylor
in 1851. [TR.]

by day and at all hours, the white tomb of his wife, and a little ease his grief.

Thus he cloistered himself, "living in memory," having no companion but the daughter of his wife; trying to console himself by work, recapitulating his life, the story of which he has told in his remarkable *Memoirs*.[28]

Fabre paid a few visits to this Thebaïd. A solitary such as Mill had become could be attracted only by a man of his temper, in whom he found, if not an affinity of nature, at least tastes like his own, and immense learning, as great as his. For Mill also was versed in all the branches of human knowledge: not only had he meditated on the high problems of history and political economy, but he had also probed all branches of science: mathematics, physics, and natural history. It was above all botany which served them as a bond of union, and they were often seen to set forth on a botanizing expedition through the countryside.

This friendship, which was not without profit for Fabre,[29] was still more precious to Mill, who found, in the society of the naturalist, a certain relief from his sorrow. The substance of their conversation was far from being such as one might have imagined it. Mill was not highly

sensible to the festival of nature or the poetry of
the fields. He was hardly interested in botany,
except from the somewhat abstract point of view
of classification and the systematic arrangement
of species. Always melancholy, cold, and
distant, he spoke little; but Fabre felt under
this apparent sensibility a rigorous integrity of
character, a great capacity for devotion, and a
rare goodness of heart.

So the two wandered across country, each
thinking his own thoughts, and each self-con-
tained as though they were walking on parallel
but distant paths.

However, Fabre was not at the end of his
troubles; and secret ill-feeling began to surround him. The free lectures at Saint-Martial
offended the devout, angered the sectaries, and
excited the intolerance of the pedants, " whose
feeble eyelids blink at the daylight," and he
was far from receiving, from his colleagues at
the *lycée*, the sympathy and encouragement
which were, at this moment especially, so necessary to him. Some even went so far as to
denounce him publicly, and he was mentioned
one day from the height of the pulpit, to the
indignation of the pupils of the upper Normal
College, as a man at once dangerous and sub-
versive.

Some found it objectionable that this "irregular person, this man of solitary study,"
should, by his work and by the magic of his
teaching, assume a position so unique and
so disproportionate. Others regarded the novelty
of placing the sciences at the disposal of young
girls as a heresy and a scandal.

Their bickering, their cabals, their secret
manœuvres, were in the long run to triumph.
Duruy had just succumbed under the incessant
attacks of the clericals. In him Fabre lost a
friend, a protector, and his only support. Em-
bittered, defeated, he was now only waiting for
a pretext, an incident, a mere nothing, to throw
up everything.

One fine morning his landladies, devout and
aged spinsters, made themselves the instruments
of the spite of his enemies, and abruptly gave
him notice to quit. He had to leave before the
end of the month, for, simple and confident as
usual, he had obtained neither a lease nor the
least written agreement.

At this moment he was so poor that he had
not even the money to meet the expenses of his
removal. The times were troublous : the great
war had commenced, and Paris being invested

he could no longer obtain the small earnings which his textbooks were beginning to yield him, and which had for some time been increasing his modest earnings. On the other hand, having always lived far from all society, he had not at Avignon a single relation who could assist him, and he could neither obtain credit nor find any one to extricate him from his embarrassments and save him from the extremity of need with which he was threatened. He thought of Mill, and in this difficult juncture it was Mill who saved him. The philosopher was then in England; he was for the time being a member of the House of Commons, and he used to vary his life at Avignon by a few weeks' sojourn in London. His reply, however, was not long in coming: almost immediately he sent help; a sum of some £120, which fell like manna into the hands of Fabre; and he did not, in exchange, demand the slightest security for this advance.

Then, filled with disgust, the " irregular person " shook off the yoke and retired to Orange. At first he took shelter where he could, anxious only to avoid as far as possible any contact with his fellow-men; then, having finally discovered a dwelling altogether in conformity with his tastes, he moved to the outskirts of the city, and settled at the edge of the fields, in the middle of a great meadow, in an isolated house, pleasant and commodious, connected with the road to Camaret by a superb avenue of tall and handsome plane-trees. This hermitage in some respects recalled that of Mill in the outskirts of Avignon ; and thence his eyes, embracing a vast horizon, from the pediment of the ancient theatre to the hills of Sérignan, could already distinguish the promised land.

V

A GREAT TEACHER

IT was in 1871. Fabre had lived twenty years
at Avignon. This date constitutes an important
landmark in his career, since it marks the precise
moment of his final rupture with the University.

At this time the preoccupations of material life
were more pressing than ever, and it was then
that he devoted himself entirely and with perseverance to the writing of those admirable
works of introduction and initiation, in which
he applied himself to rendering science accessible
to the youngest minds, and employed all his
profound knowledge to the thorough teaching of
its elements and its eternal laws.

To this ungrateful task—ungrateful, but in
reality pleasurable, so strongly had he the
vocation, the feeling, and the genius of the
teacher—Fabre applied himself thenceforth with
all his heart, and for nine years never lifted his
hand.

How insipid, how forbidding were the usual classbooks, the second-rate natural histories above all, stuffed with dry statements, with raw knowledge, which brought nothing but the memory into play! How many youthful faces had grown pale above them!

What a contrast and a deliverance in these little books of Fabre's, so clear, so luminous, so simple, which for the first time spoke to the heart and the understanding; for "work which one does not understand disgusts one." [1]

To initiate others into science or art, it is not enough to have understood them oneself; it is not enough even that one should be an artist or a scientist. Scientists of the highest flight are sometimes very unskilful teachers, and very indifferent hands at explaining the alphabet. It is not given to the first comer to educate the young; to understand how to identify his understanding with theirs, to measure their powers. It is a matter of instinct and good sense rather than of memory or erudition, and Fabre, who had never in his life been the pupil of any one, could better than any remember the phases through which his mind had passed, could recollect by what detours of the mind, by what secret labours of thought, by what intuitive methods he had succeeded in conquering, one by one, all the difficulties in his path, and in gradually attaining to knowledge.

It is wonderful to watch the mastery with which he conducts his demonstrations, the simplest as well as the most involved, singling out the essential, little by little evoking the sense of things, ingeniously seeking familiar examples, finding comparisons, and employing picturesque and striking images, which throw a dazzling light upon the obscurest question or the most difficult problem. How in such matters can one dispense with figurative speech, when one is reduced, as a rule, to an inability to show the things themselves, but only their images and their symbols?

Follow him, for example, in *The Sky*,[2] which seems to thrill with the ardent and comprehensive genius of a Humboldt, and admire the ease with which he surmounts all the difficulties and smooths the way for the vast voyage on which he conducts you, past the infinity of the suns and the stars in their millions, scintillating in the cold air of night, to descend once more to our humble *Earth;*[3] first an ocean of fire, rolling its heavy waves of molten porphyry and granite, then " slowly hardening into strange floes and

bergs, hotter than the red iron in the fire of
the forge," rounding its back, all covered with
gaping pustules, eruptive mountains and craters,
and the first folds of its calcined crust, until the
day when the vast mist of densest vapours,
heaped up on every hand and of immeasurable
depth, begins gradually to show rifts, giving
rise at last to an infinite storm, a stupendous
deluge, and forming the strange universal sea,
" a mineral sludge, veiled by a chaos of smoke,"
whence at length the primitive soil emerges,
" and at last the green grass."

And although " a little animal proteid, capable
of pleasure and pain, surpasses in interest the
whole immense creation of dead matter," he does
not forget to show us the spectacle of life flowing through matter itself ; and he animates even
the simple elementary bodies, celebrating the
marvellous activities of the air, the violence of
Chlorine, the metamorphoses of Carbon, the
miraculous bridals of Phosphorus, and " the
splendours which accompany the birth of a drop
of water." 4

A man must indeed love knowledge deeply
before he can make others love it, or render it
easy and attractive, revealing only the smiling

highways; and Fabre, above all things the impassioned professor, was the very man to lead his disciples "between the hedges of hawthorn and sloe," whether to show them the sap, "that fruitful current, that flowing flesh, that vegetable blood," or how the plant, by a mysterious transubstantiation, makes its wood, "and the delicate bundle of swaddling-bands of its buds," or how "from a putrid ordure it extracts the flavour and the fragrance of its fruits"; or whether he seeks to evoke the murderous plants that live as parasites at the cost of others; the white Clandestinus, "which strangles the roots of the alders beside the rivers," the Cuscuta, "which knows nothing of labour," the wicked Orobanche, plump, powerful and brazen, the skin covered with ugly scales, "with sombre flowers that wear the livery of death, which leaps at the throat of the clover, stifling it, devouring it, sucking its blood." [5]

Botany, by this genial treatment, becomes a most interesting study, and I know of no more captivating reading than *The Plant* and *The Story of the Log,* the jewels of this incomparable series.

Employ Fabre's method if you wish to learn by yourself, or to evoke in your children a love

of science, and, according to the phrase of the
gentle Jean-Jacques, to help them " to buy at
the best possible of prices." Give them as sole
guides these exquisite manuals, which touch upon
everything, initiating them into everything, and
bringing within the reach of all, for their instruction or amusement, the heavens and the earth,
the planets and their moons, the mechanism of
the great natural forces and the laws which
govern them, life and its materials, agriculture
and its applications. For more than a quarter
of a century these catechisms of science, models
of lucidity and good sense, effected the education
of generations of Frenchmen. Abridgments of
all knowledge, veritable codes of rural wisdom,
these perfect breviaries have never been surpassed.

It was after reading these little books, it is
said, that Duruy conceived the idea of confiding
to this admirable teacher the education of the
Imperial heir ; and it is very probable that this
was, in reality, the secret motive which would
explain why he had so expressly summoned Fabre
to Paris. What an ideal tutor he had thought
of, and how proud might others have been of
such a choice ! But the man was too zealous
of his independence, too difficult to tame, to

bear with the environment of a court, and God knows whether he was made for such refulgence ! We need not be surprised that Fabre never heard of it ; it must have sufficed the minister to speak with him for a few minutes to realize that the most tempting offers and all the powers of seduction would never overcome his insurmountable dislike of life in a capital, nor prevail against his inborn, passionate, exclusive love of the open.

For these volumes Fabre was at first rather wretchedly paid ; at all events, until public education had definitely received a fresh impulse ; and for a long time his life at Orange was literally a hand-to-mouth existence.

As soon as he was able to realize a few advances, he had nothing so much at heart as the repayment of Mill, and he hastened to call on the philosopher ; all the more filled with gratitude for his generosity in that the loan, although of the comparatively large amount of three thousand francs, was made without security, practically from hand to hand, with no other warranty than his probity.

For this reason this episode was always engraven on his memory. Thirty years later he would relate the affair even to the most insignificant details. How many times has he

not reminded me of the transaction, insisting
that I should make a note of it, so anxious was
he that this incident in his career should not be
lost in oblivion! How often has he not recalled the infinite delicacy of Mill, and his
excessive scrupulousness, which went so far that
he wished to give a written acknowledgment of
the repayment of the debt, of which there was
no record whatever save in the conscience of the
debtor!

Scarcely two years later Mill died suddenly
at Avignon. Grief finally killed him; for this
unexpected death seemed to have been only
the ultimate climax of the secret malady which
had so long been undermining him.

It was in the outskirts of Orange that Fabre
for the last time met him and accompanied him
upon a botanizing expedition. He was struck
by his weakness and his rapid decline. Mill
could hardly drag himself along, and when he
stooped to gather a specimen he had the greatest
difficulty in rising. They were never to meet
again.

A few days later—on the 8th May, 1873—
Fabre was invited to lunch with the philosopher.
Before going to the little house by the cemetery
he halted, as was his custom, at the Libraire

Saint-Just. It was there that he learned, with amazement, of the tragic and sudden event which set a so unexpected term to a friendship which was doubtless a little remote, but which was, on both sides, a singularly lofty and beautiful attachment.

His class-books were now bringing in scarcely anything; their preparation, moreover, involved an excessive expenditure of time, and gave him a great deal of trouble; it is impossible to imagine what scrupulous care, what zeal and self-respect Fabre brought to the execution of the programme which he had to fulfil.

To begin with, he considered that he could not enjoy a more splendid opportunity to give children a taste for science and to stimulate their curiosity than by finding a means to interest them, from their earliest infancy, in their simple playthings, even the crudest and most inexpensive; so true is it that " in the smallest mechanical device or engine, even in its simplest form, as conceived by the industry of a child, there is often the germ of important truths, and, better than books, the school of the playroom, if gently disciplined, will open for the child the windows of the universe."

" The humble teetotum, made of a crust of

rye-bread transfixed by a twig, silently spinning on the cover of a school-book, will give a correct enough image of the earth, which retains unmoved its original impulse, and travels along a great circle, at the same time turning on itself. Gummed on its disc, scraps of paper properly coloured will tell us of white light, decomposable into various coloured rays. . . .

" There will be the pop-gun, with its ramrod and its two plugs of tow, the hinder one expelling the foremost by the elasticity of the compressed air. Thus we get a glimpse of the ballistics of gunpowder, and the pressure of steam in engines. . . ."

The little hydraulic fountain made of an apricot stone, patiently hollowed and pierced with a hole at either side, into which two straws are fitted, one dipping into a cup of water and the other duly capped, " expelling a slender thread of water in which the sunlight flickers," will introduce us to the true syphon of physics.

" What amusing and useful lessons " a well-balanced scheme of education might extract from this " academy of childish ingenuity " ! [6]

At this time he was undertaking the education of his own children. His chemistry lessons especially had a great success.[7] With apparatus of his own devising and of the simplest kind, he could perform a host of elementary experiments, the apparatus as a rule consisting of the most ordinary materials, such as a common flask or bottle, an old mustard-pot, a tumbler, a goose-quill or a pipe-stem.

A series of astonishing phenomena amazed their wondering eyes. He made them see, touch, taste, handle, and smell, and always " the hand assisted the word," always " the example accompanied the precept," for no one more fully valued the profound maxim, so neglected and misunderstood, that " to see is to know."

He exerted himself to arouse their curiosity, to provoke their questions, to discover their mistakes, to set their ideas in order ; he accustomed them to rectify their errors themselves, and from all this he obtained excellent material for his books.

For those more especially intended for the education of girls he took counsel with his daughter Antonia, inviting her collaboration, begging her to suggest every aspect of the matter that occurred to her ; for instance, in respect of the chemistry of the household, " where exact science should shed its light upon a host of facts relating to domestic economy," [8] from the washing of clothes to the making of a stew.

Even now, to his despair, although freed
from the cares of school life, he was always
almost wholly without leisure to devote himself
to his chosen subjects.

It was at this period above all that he felt
so " lonely, abandoned, struggling against misfortune ; and before one can philosophize one
has to live." 9

And his incessant labour was aggravated by
a bitter disappointment. In the year of Mill's
death Fabre was dismissed from his post as conservator of the Requien Museum, which he had
held in spite of his departure from Avignon, going
thither regularly twice a week to acquit himself
of his duties. The municipality, working in the
dark, suddenly dismissed him without explanation. To Fabre this dismissal was infinitely
bitter ; " a sweeper-boy would have been treated
with as much ceremony." 10   What afflicted
him most was not the undeserved slight of the
dismissal, but his unspeakable regret at quitting
those beloved vegetable collections, " amassed
with such love " by Requien, who was his friend
and master, and by Mill and himself ; and the
thought that he would henceforth perhaps be
unable to save these precious but perishable
things from oblivion, or terminate the botanical
geography of Vaucluse, on which he had been
thirty years at work !

For this reason, when there was some talk of establishing an agronomic station at Avignon, and of appointing him director, he was at first warmly in favour of the idea.[11] Already he foresaw a host of fascinating experiments, of the highest practical value, conducted in the peace and leisure and security of a fixed appointment. It is indeed probable that in so vast a field he would have demonstrated many valuable truths, fruitful in practical results; he was certainly meant for such a task, and he would have performed it with genuine personal satisfaction. He had already exerted his ingenuity by trying to develop, among the children of the countryside, a taste for agriculture, which he rightly considered the logical complement of the primary school, and which is based upon all the sciences which he himself had studied, probed, taught, and popularized.

It will be remembered how patiently he devoted himself for twelve years to the study of madder, multiplying his researches, and applying himself not only to extracting the colouring principle, but also to indicating means whereby adulteration and fraud might be detected.

He had published memoirs of great importance dealing with entomology in its relations to agriculture. Impressed with the importance of this little world, he suggested valuable remedies, means of preservation ; which were all the more logical in that the destruction of insects, if it is to be efficacious, must be based not upon a gross empiricism, but on a previous study of their social life and their habits.

With what patience he observed the terribly destructive weevils, and those formidable moths with downy wings, which fly without sound of a night, and whose depredations have often been valued at millions of francs ! How meticulously he has recorded the conditions which favour or check the development of those parasitic fungi whose mortal blemishes are seen on buds and flowers, on the green shoots and clusters that promise a prosperous vintage !

But then he became anxious. Was it all worth the sacrifice of his liberty? " Would he not suffer a thousand annoyances from pretentious nobodies? " for as things were, all ideas of again " enregimenting " himself " filled him with horror." [12]

Slowly, however, the first instalment of the work which he had spent nearly twenty-five years in planning, creating, and polishing, began to take shape. At the end of the year 1878 he was able to assemble a sufficient number of studies to form material for what was to be the first volume of his *Souvenirs entomologiques*.*

Let us stop for a moment to consider this first book, whose publication constitutes a truly historical date, not only in the career of Fabre, but in the annals of universal science. It was at once the foundation and the keystone of the marvellous edifice which we shall watch unfolding and increasing, but to which the future was in reality to add nothing essential. The cardinal ideas as to instinct and evolution, the necessity of experimenting in the psychology of animals, and the harmonic laws of the conservation of the individual, are here already expounded in their final and definite form. This fruitful and decisive year brought Fabre a great grief. He lost his son Jules, that one of all his children whom he seems most ardently to have loved.

He was a youth of great promise, " all fire, all flame "; of a serious nature ; an exquisite being, of a precocious intelligence, whose rare aptitudes both for science and literature were truly extraordinary. Such too was the subtlety of his senses that by handling no matter what plant, with his eyes closed, he could recognize and define it merely by the sense of touch. This

* A selection of which forms *Social Life in the Insect World* (The Century Co., 1912).

delightful companion of his father's studies had scarcely passed his fifteenth year when death removed him. A terrible void was left in his heart, which was never filled. Thirty years later the least allusion to this child, however tactful, which recalled this dear memory to his mind, would still wring his heart, and his whole body would be shaken by his sobs. As always, work was his refuge and consolation ; but this terrible blow shattered his health, until then so robust. In the midst of this disastrous winter he fell seriously ill. He was stricken with pneumonia, which all but carried him off, and every one gave him up for lost. However, he recovered, and issued from his convalescence as though regenerated, and with strength renewed he attacked the next stage of his labours.

But what are the most fruitful resolutions, and what poor playthings are we in the hands of the unexpected ! A vulgar incident of every-day life had sufficed to make Fabre decide to break openly with the University, and to leave Avignon. The secret motive of his departure from Orange was scarcely more solid. His new landlord concluded one day, either from cupidity or stupidity, to lop most ferociously the two magnificent rows of plane-trees which formed a shady avenue before his house, in which the birds piped and

warbled in the spring, and the cicadæ chorused
in the summer. Fabre could not endure this
massacre, this barbarous mutilation, this crime
against nature. Hungry for peace and quiet,
the enjoyment of a dwelling-place could no
longer content him ; at all costs he must own
his own home.

So, having won the modest ransom of his
deliverance, he waited no longer, but quitted the
cities for ever ; retiring to Sérignan, to the
peaceful obscurity of a tiny hamlet, and this
quiet corner of the earth had henceforth all his
heart and soul in keeping.

VI

THE HERMITAGE

GOETHE has somewhere written: Whosoever would understand the poet and his work should visit the poet's country.

Let us, then, the latest of many, make the pilgrimage which all those who are fascinated by the enigma of nature will accomplish later, with the same piety that has led so many and so fervent admirers to the dwelling of Mistral at Maillane.

Starting from Orange and crossing the Aygues, a torrent whose muddy waters are lost in the Rhône, but whose bed is dried by the July and August suns, leaving only a desert of pebbles, where the mason-bee builds her pretty turrets of rock-work, we come presently to the Sérignaise country; an arid, stony tract, planted with vines and olives, coloured a rusty red, or touched here and there with almost the hue of blood; and here and there a grove of cypress makes a sombre blot. To the north runs a long black line of hills, covered with box and ilex and the giant heather of the south. Far in the distance, to the east, the immense plain is closed in by the wall of Saint-Amant and the ridge of the Dentelle, behind which the lofty Ventoux rears its rocky, cloven bosom abruptly to the clouds. At the end of a few miles of dusty road, swept by the powerful breath of the mistral, we suddenly reach a little village. It is a curious little community, with its central street adorned by a double row of plane-trees, its leaping fountains, and its almost Italian air. The houses are lime-washed, with flat roofs; and sometimes, at the side of some small or decrepit dwelling, we see the unexpected curves of a loggia. At a distance the façade of the church has the harmonious lines of a little antique temple; close at hand is the graceful campanile, an old octagonal tower surmounted by a narrow mitre wrought in hammered iron, in the midst of which are seen the black profiles of the bells.

I shall never forget my first visit. It was in the month of August; and the whole country-side was ringing with the song of the cicadæ. I had applied to a job-master of Orange, count-

ing on him to take me thither ; but he had never
driven any one to Sérignan, had hardly heard of
Fabre, and did not know where his house was.
At length, however, we contrived to find it. At
the entrance of the little market-town, in a
solitary corner, in the centre of an enclosure of
lofty walls, which were taller than the crests of
the pines and cypresses, his dwelling was hidden
away. No sound proceeded from it ; but for
the baying of the faithful Tom I do not think I
should have dared to knock on the great door,
which turned slowly on its hinges. A pink house
with green shutters, half-hidden amid the sombre
foliage, appears at the end of an alley of lilacs,
" which sway in the spring under the weight of
their balmy thyrsi." Before the house are the
shady plane-trees, where during the burning
hours of August the cicada of the flowering ash,
the deafening *cacan*, concealed beneath the
leaves, fills the hot atmosphere with its eager
cries, the only sound that disturbs the profound
silence of this solitude.

Before us, beyond a little wall of a height to
lean upon, on an isolated lawn, beneath the shade
of great trees with interwoven boughs, a circular basin displays its still surface, across which
the skating Hydrometra traces its wide circles.

Then, suddenly, we see an opening into the most extraordinary and unexpected of gardens ; a wild park, full of strenuous vegetation, which hides the pebbly soil in all directions ; a chaos of plants and bushes, created throughout especially to attract the insects of the neighbourhood.

Thickets of wild laurel and dense clumps of lavender encroach upon the paths, alternating with great bushes of coronilla, which bar the flight of the butterfly with their yellow-winged flowers, and whose searching fragrance embalms all the air about them.

It is as though the neighbouring mountain had one day departed, leaving here its thistles, its dogberry-trees, its brooms, its rushes, its juniper-bushes, its laburnums, and its spurges. There too grows the " strawberry-tree," whose red fruits wear so familiar an appearance ; and tall pines, the giants of this " pigmy forest." There the Japanese privet ripens its black berries, mingled with the Paulownia and the Cratœgus with their tender green foliage. Coltsfoot mingles with violets ; clumps of sage and thyme mix their fragrance with the scent of rosemary and a host of balsamic plants. Amid the cacti, their fleshy leaves bristling with prickles, the periwinkle opens its scattered blossoms, while in a corner the serpent arum raises its cornucopia, in which those insects that love putrescence fall engulfed, deceived by the horrible savour of its exhalations.

It is in the spring above all that one should see this torrent of verdure, when the whole enclosure awakens in its festival attire, decked with all the flowers of May, and the warm air, full of the hum of insects, is perfumed with a thousand intoxicating scents. It is in the spring that one should see the " Harmas," the open-air observatory, " the laboratory of living ento-mology " [1] ; a name and a spot which Fabre has made famous throughout the world.

I enter the dining-room, whose wide, half-closed shutters allow only a half-light to enter between the printed curtains. Rush-bottomed chairs, a great table, about which seven persons daily take their places, a few poor pieces of furniture, and a simple bookcase ; such are all the contents. On the mantel, a clock in black marble, a precious souvenir, the only present which Fabre received at the time of his exodus from Avignon ; it was given by his old pupils, the young girls who used to attend the free lectures at Saint-Martial's.

There, every afternoon, half lying on a little sofa, the naturalist has the habit of taking a short siesta. This light repose, even without sleep, was of old enough to restore his energies, exhausted by hours of labour. Thenceforth he was once more alert, and ready for the remainder of the day.

But already he is on his feet, bareheaded, in his waistcoat, his silk necktie carelessly fastened under the soft turned-down collar of his half-open shirt, his gesture, in the shadowy chamber, full of welcome.

François Sicard, in his faultless medal and his admirable bust, has succeeded with rare felicity in reproducing for posterity this rugged, shaven face, full of laborious years ; a peasant face, stamped with originality, under the wide felt hat of Provence ; touched with geniality and benevolence, yet reflecting a world of energy. Sicard has fixed for ever this strange mask ; the thin cheeks, ploughed into deep furrows, the strained nose, the pendent wrinkles of the throat, the thin, shrivelled lips, with an indescribable fold of bitterness at the corners of the mouth. The hair, tossed back, falls in fine curls over the ears, revealing a high, rounded forehead, obstinate and full of thought. But what chisel, what graver could reproduce the surprising shrewdness of that gaze, eclipsed from time to time by a convulsive tremor of the eyelids !

What Holbein, what Chardin could render the
almost extraordinary brilliance of those black
eyes, those dilated pupils : the eyes of a prophet,
a seer ; singularly wide and deeply set, as though
gazing always upon the mystery of things, as
though made expressly to scrutinize Nature and
decipher her enigmas?   Above the orbits, two
short, bristling eyebrows seem set there to guide
the vision ; one, by dint of knitting itself above
the magnifying-glass, has retained an indelible
fold of continual attention ; the other, on the
contrary, always updrawn, has the look of defy-
ing the interlocutor, of foreseeing his objections,
of waiting with an ever-ready return-thrust.
Such is this striking physiognomy, which one
who has seen it cannot forget.

There, in this " hermit's retreat," as he himself has defined it, the sage is voluntarily seques-
tered ; a true saint of science, an ascetic living
only on fruits, vegetables, and a little wine ;
so in love with retirement that even in the village
he was for a long time almost unknown, so
careful was he to go round instead of through
it on his way to the neighbouring mountain,
where he would often spend whole days alone
with wild nature.

It is in this silent Thebaïd, so far from
the atmosphere of cities, the vain agitations and

storms of the world, that his life has been passed, in unchanging uniformity ; and here he has been able to pursue, with resolute labour and incredible patience, that prodigious series of marvellous observations which for nearly fifty years he has never ceased to accumulate.

Let us indeed remember how much time has been required and what effort has been expended to complete the long and patient inquiries which he had hitherto accomplished ; obliged, as he was, to allow himself to be interrupted at any moment, and to postpone his observations often at the most interesting moment, in order to undertake some enervating labour, or the disagreeable and mechanical duties of his profession. Remember that his first labours already dated from twenty-five years earlier, and at the moment when we observe him in his solitude at Sérignan he had only just painfully gathered together the material for his first book. What a contrast to the thirty fruitful years that were to follow ! Now nearly ten volumes, no less overflowing with the richest material, were to succeed one another at almost regular intervals—about one in every three years.

To be sure, he would have gathered his harvest in no matter what corner of the world, provided he had found within his reach, in whatever sphere

of life he had been placed, any subject of inquiry
whatever ; such was Rousseau, botanizing over
the bunch of chickweed provided for his canary ;
such was Bernardin Saint-Pierre, discovering a
world in a strawberry-plant which had sprouted
by chance at the corner of his window.[2] But the
field in which he had hitherto been able to glean
was indeed barren.   That he was able, later on,
to narrate the wonderful history of the Pelopæus,
whose habits he had observed at Avignon, was
due to the fact that this curious insect had come
to lodge with him, having chosen Fabre's
chamber for its dwelling.   None the less he
threw himself eagerly upon all such scraps of
information as happened to come under his
notice ; witness the observations which he
embodied in a memoir touching the phosphorescence of certain earth-worms which,
abounding in a little courtyard near his
dwelling, were so rare elsewhere that he was
never again able to find them.[3]   It was therefore
fortunate, if not for himself, at least for his
genius, that he did not become, as he had wished,
a professor in a faculty ; there, to be sure, he
would have found a theatre worthy of his efforts,
in which he might even have demonstrated, in
all its magnificence, his incomparable gift of
teaching ; but it is probable too that he would

have been stranded in shoal waters ; that in the official atmosphere of a city his still more marvellous gifts of observation would scarcely have found employment.

It was only by belonging fully to himself that he could fruitfully exercise his talents. Necessary to every scholar, to every inquirer, to an open-air observer like Fabre liberty and leisure were more than usually essential ; failing these he might never have accomplished his mission. How many lives are wasted, how many minds expended in sheer loss, in default of this sufficiency of leisure ! How many scholars tied to the soil, how many physicians absorbed by an exigent practice, who perhaps had somewhat to say, have succeeded only in devising plans, for ever postponing their realization to some miraculous to-morrow, which always recedes !

But we must not fall into illusions. How many might be tempted to imitate him, hoping to see some unknown talent awaken or expand within them, only to find themselves incapable of producing anything, and to consume themselves in an insurmountable and barren ennui ! One must be rich in one's own nature, rich in will and in ability, to live apart and seek new paths in solitude, and it is not without reason that the majority prefer the turmoil of cities and the murmur of men to the silence of the country.

The atmosphere of a great capital, for instance, is singularly conducive to work. Living constantly within the circle of light shed by the masters, within reach of the laboratories and the great libraries, we are less likely to go astray; we are stimulated by the contact of others; we profit by their advice and experience; and it is easy to borrow ideas if we lack them. Then there is the stimulant of self-respect, the sense of rivalry, the eager desire to advance, to distinguish oneself, to shine, to attract attention, to become in one's turn an arbiter, an object of wonder and envy, without which stimulus many would merely have existed, and would never have become what they are.

On the other hand, a man needs an intrinsic *radio-activity*, and a real talent; and the aid, moreover, of exceptional circumstances, if fame is to consent to come to him and take him by the hand in the depths of some unknown Maillane, some obscure Sérignan; even, as in the case of Fabre, at the end only of a long life.

But he, by a kind of fatality inherent in his

nature, loved " to circumscribe himself," according to the happy expression of Rousseau ; and
he profited, rather than otherwise, by living
entirely to himself ; for he had long been, indeed
he always was, the man who, at twenty-five,
writing to his brother, had said, in speaking of
his native countryside :

" For an impassioned botanist, it is a delightful country, in which I could pass a month,
two months, three months, a year even, alone,
quite alone, with no other companion than the
crows and the jays which gossip among the oak-
trees ; without being weary for a moment ; there
would be so many beautiful fungi, orange, rosy,
and white, among the mosses, and so many
flowers in the fields." [4]

His work having brought him at last just
enough to enable him to give himself the pleasure
of becoming, in his turn, a proprietor, he had
acquired, for a modest sum, this dilapidated
dwelling and this deserted spot of ground ;
barren land, given over to couch-grass, thistles,
and brambles ; a sort of " accursed spot, to
which no one would have confided even a pinch
of turnip-seed." A piece of water in front of
the house attracted all the frogs in the neighbourhood ; the screech-owl mewed from the tops

of the plane-trees, and numerous birds, no longer disturbed by the presence of man, had domiciled themselves in the lilacs and the cypresses. A host of insects had seized upon the dwelling, which had long been deserted.

He restored the house, and to some extent reduced confusion to order. In the uncultivated and pebbly plain where the plough had been long a stranger he established plants of a thousand varieties, and, the better to hide himself, he had walls built to shut himself in.

Why was he drawn by preference to this village of Sérignan?—for he did not go thither without making some inquiries as to the possibility of obtaining shelter elsewhere, and the Carpentras cemetery had tempted him also ; but what had particularly seduced and drawn him thither was the nearness of the mountain with its Mediterranean flora, so rich that it recalled the Corsican *maquis* ; full of beautiful fungi and varied insects, where, under the flat stones exposed to the burning sun, the centipede burrowed and the scorpion slept ; where a special fauna abounded—of curious dung-beetles, scarabæi, the Copris, the Minotaur, etc.—which only a little farther north grow rapidly scarcer and then altogether disappear.

He had thus at last arrived in port; he had found his " Eden."

He had realized, " after forty years of desperate struggles," the dearest, the most ardent, the longest cherished of all his desires. He could observe at leisure " every day, every hour," his beloved insects; " under the blue sky, to the music of the cigales." He had only to open his eyes and to see; to lend an ear and hear; to enjoy the great blessing of leisure to his heart's content.

Doffing the professor's frock-coat for the peasant's blouse, planting a root of sweet basil in his " topper," and finally kicking it to pieces, he snapped his fingers at his past life.

Liberated at last, far from all that could irritate or disturb him or make him feel dependent, satisfied with his modest earnings, reassured by the ever-increasing popularity of his little books, he had obtained entire possession of his own body and mind, and could give himself without reserve to his favourite subjects.

So, with Nature and her inexhaustible book before him, he truly commenced a new life.

But would this life have been possible without the support and comfort of those intimate feelings which are at the root of human nature? Man is seldom the master of these feelings, and they, with reason or despite reason, force themselves on his notice as the question of questions.

This delicate problem Fabre had to resolve after suffering a fresh grief. Hardly had he commenced to enjoy the benefits of this profound peace, when he lost his wife. At this moment his children were already grown up ; some were married and some ready to leave him ; and he could not hope much longer to keep his old father, the ex-café-keeper of Pierrelatte, who had come to rejoin him, and who might be seen, even in his extreme old age, going forth in all weathers and dragging his aged limbs along all the roads of Sérignan.5 The son, moreover, had inherited from his father his profound inaptitude for the practical business of life, and was equally incapable of managing his interests and the economics of the house. This is why, after two years of widowerhood, having already passed his sixtieth year, although still physically quite youthful, he remarried. Careless of opinion, obeying only the dictates of his own heart and mind, and following also the intuitions of unerring instinct, which was superior to the understanding of those who thought it their duty to oppose him, he married, as Boaz married Ruth, a young woman, industrious, full of fresh-

ness and life, already completely devoted to his
service, and admirably fitted to satisfy that crav-
ing for order, peace, quiet, and moral tranquillity,
which to him were above all things indispensable.

His new companion, moreover, was in all
things faithful to her mission, and it was thanks
to the benefits of this union, as the future was to
show, that Fabre was in a position to pursue his
long-delayed inquiries.

Three children, a son and two daughters, were
born in swift succession, and reconstituted " the
family," which was very soon increased by the
youngest of his daughters by his first wife, who
had not married ; this was that Aglaë, who so
often helped her father with her childlike attentions, and, " her cheek blooming with animation,"
collaborated in some of his most famous observations ; 6 an unobtrusive figure, a soul full of
devotion and resignation, heroic and tender.
Having in vain ventured into the world, she
had returned to the beloved roof at Sérignan,
unable to part from the father she so admired
and adored.

Later, when the shadow of age grew denser
and heavier, the young wife and the younger
children of the famous poet-entomologist took
part in his labours also ; they gave him their

material assistance, their hands, their eyes, their hearing, their feet; he in the midst of them was the conceiving, reasoning, interpreting, and directing brain.

From this time forward the biography of Fabre becomes simplified, and remains a statement of his inner life. For thirty years he never emerged from his horizon of mountains and his garden of shingle; he lived wholly absorbed in domestic affections and the tasks of a naturalist. None the less, he still exercised his vocation as teacher, for neither pure science nor poetry was sufficient to nourish his mind, and he was still Professor Fabre, untiringly pursuing his programme of education, although no longer applying himself thereto exclusively.

This long active period was also the most silent period of his life, although not an hour, not a minute of his many days was left unoccupied.

In the first few months at his new home he resumed his hymn to labour.

" You will learn in your turn," he writes to his son Émile, " you will learn, I hope, that we are never so happy as when work does not leave us a moment's repose. To act is to live." 7

The better to belong to himself, he eluded all invitations, even those from his nearest or most intimate friends ; he hated to go away even for a few hours, preferring to enjoy in his own house their presence amidst his habitual and delightful surroundings. Everything in this still unexplored country was new to him. What would he do elsewhere, even in his beloved Carpentras, whither his faithful friend and pupil Devillario, who had formerly followed him in his walks around Avignon, would endeavour from time to time to draw him ? Devillario was a magistrate, a collector and palæontologist ; his simple tastes, his wide culture, and his passion for natural history would surely have decided Fabre to accept his invitations, but that he forbade himself the pleasure. " I am afraid the hospitable cutlet that awaits me at your table will have time to grow cold ; I am up to the neck in my work.[8] . . . But you, when you can, escape from your courts, and we will philosophize at random, as is our custom when we can manage to pass a few hours together. As for me, it is very doubtful whether the temptation will seize me to come to Carpentras. A hermit of the Thebaïd was no more diligent in his cell than I in my village home." [9]

VII

THE INTERPRETATION OF NATURE

WAS there not indeed a sufficiency of captivating matters all about him, and beneath his very feet?

In his deep, sunny garden a thousand insects fly, creep, crawl, and hum, and each relates its history to him. A golden gardener-beetle trots along the path. Rose-beetles pass, in snoring flight, on every hand, the gold and emerald of their elytra gleaming; now and again one of them alights for a moment on the flowering head of a thistle; he seizes it carefully with the tips of his nervous, pointed fingers, seems to caress it, speaks to it, and then suddenly restores it to freedom.

Wasps are pillaging the centauries. On the blossoms of the camomile the larvæ of the Meloë are waiting for the Anthophoræ to carry them off to their cells, while around them roam the Cicindelæ, their green bodies "spotted with points of amaranth." At the bottom of the walls

" the chilly Psyche creeps slowly along under her cloak of tiny twigs." In the dead bough of a lilac-tree the dark-hued Xylocopa, the wood-boring bee, is busy tunnelling her gallery. In the shade of the rushes the Praying Mantis, rustling the floating robe of her long tender green wings, " gazes alertly, on the watch, her arms folded on her breast, her appearance that of one praying," and paralyses the great grey locust, nailed to its place by fear.

Nothing here is insignificant ; what the world would smile at or deride will provide the sage with food for thought and reflection. " Nothing is trivial in the majestic problem of nature ; our laboratory acquaria are of less value than the imprint which the shoe of a mule has left in the clay, when the rain has filled the primitive basin, and life has peopled it with marvels " ; and the least fact offered us by chance on the most thoroughly beaten track may possibly open prospects as vast as all the starry sky.

Tell yourself that everything in nature is a symbol of something like a specimen of an abstruse cryptogram, all the characters of which conceal some meaning. But when we have suc-ceeded in deciphering these living texts, and have grasped the allusion ; when, beside the symbol,

we have succeeded in finding the commentary,
then the most desolate corner of the earth
appears to the solitary seeker as a gallery full
of the masterpieces of an unsuspected art. Fabre
puts into our hands the golden key which opens
the doors of this marvellous museum.

Let us consider the terebinth louse ; it is just
a little yellow mite ; but is it nothing else?   Its
genealogical history teaches us "by what amazing
essays of passion and variety the universal law
which rules the transmission of life is evolved.
Here is neither father nor eggs ; all these mites
are mothers ; and the young are born living,
just like their mothers."   To this end " almost
the whole of the maternal substance is disin-
tegrated and renewed and conglobated to form
the ovarium . . . the whole creature has become
an egg, which has, for its shell, the dry skin of
the tiny creature, and the microscope will show a
whole world in formation . . . a nebulosity as
of white of egg, in which fresh centres of life are
forming, as the suns are condensed in the nebulæ
of the heavens." [1]

What is this fleck of foam, like a drop of saliva,
which we see in springtime on the weeds of the
meadows ; among others on the spurge, when
its stems begin to shoot, and its sombre flowers

open in the sunlight? " It is the work of an insect.
It is the shelter in which the Cicadellina deposits
her eggs.   What a miraculous chemist!   Her
stiletto excels the finest craft of the botanical
anatomist" by its sovereign art of separating
the acrid poison which flows with the sap in the
veins of the most venomous plants, and extracting
therefrom only an inoffensive fluid.²

At every step the insects set us problems
equally varied.   The other creatures are nearer
to us ; they resemble us in many respects.   But
insects, almost the first-born of creation, form
a world apart, and contain, in their tiny bodies,
as Réaumur has admirably said, " more parts
than the most gigantic animals."   They have
senses and faculties of their own, which enable
them to accomplish actions, which are doubtless
very simply related in reality, but which seem, to
our minds, as extraordinary as the habits of the
inhabitants of Mars might, if by chance they were
to descend in our midst.   We do not know how
they hear, nor how they see through their com-
pound eyes, and our ignorance concerning the
majority of their senses still further increases the
difficulty, which so often arrests us, of interpreting
their actions.

The tubercled Cerceris " finds by the hundred " and almost immediately a species of

weevil, the *Cleona ophthalmica,* on which it feeds its larvæ, and which the human eye, though it searches for hours, can scarcely find anywhere. The eyes of the Cerceris are like magnifying glasses, veritable microscopes, which immediately distinguish, in the vast field of nature, an object that human vision is powerless to discover.[3]

How does the Ammophila, hovering over the turf and investigating it far and wide, in its search for a grey grub, contrive to discern the precise point in the depth of the subsoil where the larva is slumbering in immobility? " Neither touch nor sight can come into play, for the grub is sealed up in its burrow at a depth of several inches; nor the scent, since it is absolutely inodorous; nor the hearing, since its immobility is absolute during the daytime." [4]

The Processional caterpillar of the pine-trees, " endowed with an exquisite hygrometric sensibility," is a barometer more infallible than that of the physicists. " It foresees the tempests preparing afar, at enormous distances, almost in the other hemisphere," and announces them several days before the least sign of them appears on the horizon.[5]

A wild bee, the Chalicodoma, and a wasp, the Cerceris, carried in the dark far from their familiar pastures, to a distance of several miles, and released in spots which they have never seen, cross vast and unknown spaces with absolute certainty, and regain their nests ; even after long absence, and in spite of contrary winds and the most unexpected obstacles. It is not memory that guides them, but a special faculty whose astonishing results we must admit without attempting to explain them, so far removed are they from our own psychology.[6] But here is another example :

The Greater Peacock moths cross hills and valleys in the darkness, with a heavy flight of wings spotted with inexplicable hieroglyphics. They hasten from the remotest depths of the horizon to find their " sleeping beauties," drawn thereto by unknown odours, inappreciable by our senses, yet so penetrating that the branch of almond on which the female has perched, and which she has impregnated with her effluvium, exerts the same extraordinary attraction.[7]

Considering these creatures, we end by discovering more things than are contained in all the philosophies . . . if we know how to look for them.

Among so many unimaginable phenomena, which bewilder us, " because there is nothing analogous in us," we succeed in perceiving, here and there, a few glimpses of day, which suddenly throw a singular light upon this black labyrinth, in which the least secret we can surprise " enters perhaps more directly into the profound enigma of our ends and our origins than the secret of the most urgent and most closely studied of our passions." [8]

Fabre explains by hypnosis one of those curious facts which have hitherto been so poorly interpreted. When surprised by abnormal conditions, we see insects suddenly fall over, drop to the ground, and lie as though struck by lightning, gathering their limbs under their bodies. A shock, an unexpected odour, a loud noise, plunges them instantly into a sort of lethargy, more or less prolonged. The insect " feigns death," not because it simulates death, but in reality because this *magnetic* condition resembles that of death.[9] Now the Odynerus, the Anthidium, the Eucera, the Ammophila, and all the hymenoptera which Fabre has observed sleeping at the fall of night, " suspended in space solely by the strength of their mandibles, their bodies tense, their limbs retracted, without exhaustion or collapse "; and the larva of the Empusa, " which for some ten months hangs to a twig by its limbs, head downwards " : do not these present a surprising analogy with those hypnotized persons who possess the faculty of remaining fixed in the most painful poses, and of supporting the most unusual attitudes, for an extremely long time ; for instance, with one arm extended, or one foot raised from the ground, without appearing to experience the least fatigue, and with a persevering and unfaltering energy ? [10]

That the ex-schoolmaster was able to penetrate so far into this new world, and that he has been able to interest us in so many fascinating problems, was due to the fact that he had also " taken a wide bird's-eye view through all the windows of creation." His universal capabilities, his immense culture and almost encyclopædic science have enabled him to utilize, thanks to his studies, all the knowledge allied to his subject. He is not one of those who understand only their speciality and who, knowing nothing outside their own province and their particular labours, refuse to grasp at anything beyond the narrow limits within which they stand installed.

All plants are to him so familiar that the flowers, for him, assume the airs of living persons. But without a profound knowledge of botany, who would hope to grasp the profound, perpetual, and intimate relations of the plant and the insect?

He has turned over strata and interrogated the schistous deposits, whose archives preserve the forms of vanished organizations, but "keep silence as to the origin of the instincts." Bending over his reagents, he has sought to discover, according to the phrase of a philosopher, those secret retreats in which Nature is seated before her furnaces, in the depths of her laboratory; following up the metamorphoses of matter even to the wings of the Scarabæi, and observing how life, returning to her crucible the debris and ashes of the organism, combines the elements anew, and from the elements of the urine can derive, for example, by a simple displacement of molecules, "all this dazzling magic of colours of innumerable shades: the amethystine violet of Geotrupes, the emerald of the rose-beetle, the gilded green of the Cantharides, the metallic lustre of the gardener-beetles, and all the pomp of the Buprestes and the dung-beetles." [11]

His books are steeped in all the ideas of modern physics. The highest mathematical knowledge has been referred to with profit in his marvellous description of the hunting-net of the Epeïra, whose "terribly scientific" combinations realize "the spiral logarithm of the

geometers, so curious in its properties " ; [12] a
splendid observation, in which Fabre makes us
admire, in the humble web of a spider, a masterpiece as astonishing and incomprehensible as and
even more sublime than the honeycomb.

This explains why Fabre has always ener-
getically denied that he is properly speaking an
entomologist; and indeed the term appears
often wrongly to describe him. He loves, on
the contrary, to call himself a naturalist; that is,
a biologist; biology being, by definition, the study
of living creatures considered as a whole and
from every point of view. And as nothing in
life is isolated, as all things hold together, and
as each part, in all its relations, presents itself
to the gaze of the observer under innumerable
aspects, one cannot be a true naturalist without
being at the same time a philosopher.

But it is not enough to know and to observe.

To be admitted to the spectacle of these
tiny creatures, to become familiar with their
habits, to grasp the mysterious threads which
connect them one with another and with the
vast universe: for this the cold and deliberate
vision of the specialist would often be insufficient. There is an art of observation, and the
gift of observation is a true function of that
constantly alert intelligence, continually domi-

nated by the need of delving untiringly down
to the ultimate truth accessible, "allowing ourselves to pass over nothing without seeking its
reason, and habitually following up every
response with another question, until we come
to the granite wall of the Unknowable." Above
all we need an ardent and interested sympathy,
for " we penetrate farther into the secret of
things by the heart than by the reason," as
Toussenel has said ; and " it is only by intuition
that we can know what life truly is," adds
Bergson profoundly.[13]   Now Fabre loves these
little peoples and knows how to make us love
them.   How tenderly he speaks of them ; with
what solicitude he observes them ; with what
love he follows the progress of their nurslings ;
the young grubs wriggling in his test-tubes, with
doddering heads, are happy ; and he himself
is happy to see them " well-fed and shining with
health."   He pities the bee stabbed by the
Philanthus " in the holy joys of labour."   He
sympathizes with the sufferings of these little
creatures and their hard labours.   If, in his
search for ideas, he has to overturn their
dwellings, " he repents of subjecting maternal
love to such tribulations," and if he is constrained
to put them to the question, to torment them
in order to extract their secrets, he is grieved

to have provoked "such miseries!" [14] Having
provided for their needs, and satisfied with the
secrets which they have revealed to him, it is
not without regret and difficulty that he parts
from them and restores them "to the delights
of liberty."

He is thoroughly convinced, moreover, that
all the creatures that share the face of the earth
with us are accomplishing an august and
appointed task. He welcomes the swallows to
his dwelling, even surrendering his workroom
to them, at the risk of jeopardizing his notes
and books. He pleads for the frog, and applies
himself to setting forth his unknown qualities;
he rehabilitates the bat, the hedgehog, and the
screech-owl, persecuted, defamed, crushed,
stoned, and crucified! [15]

So intimate is the life which he leads among
them all that he makes himself truly their companion, and relates his own history in narrating
theirs; pleased to discover in their joys and
sorrows his own trials and delights; mingling
in their annals his memories and his impressions;
delightful fragments of a childlike autobiography,
encrusted in his learned work; moving and delightful pages in which all the ingenuity of this
noble mind reveals itself with a touching
sincerity, in which all the freshness of this

charming and so profoundly unworldly nature is seen as through a pure crystal.

There is no real communion with nature without sentiment, without an illuminating passion : often the sole and effectual grace which enables its true meaning to appear. Neither taste, nor intelligence, nor logic, nor all the science of the schools can suffice alone. To see further there is needed something like a gift of correspondence, surpassing the limits of observation and experience, which enables us to foresee and to divine the profound secrets of life which lie beneath appearances. Those who are so gifted have often only to open their eyes in order to grasp matters in their true light.

A great observer is in reality a poet who imagines and creates. The microscope, the magnifying glass, the scalpel, are as it were the strings of a lyre. " The felicitous and fruitful hypothesis which constitutes scientific invention is a gift of sentiment " in the words of Claude Bernard ; and of this king of physiology, who commenced by proving himself in works of pure imagination, and whose genius finally took for its theme the manifold variations of living flesh, of him too may we not say that he has explored the labyrinths of life with " the torch of poetry in his hand "?

Similarly, do not the harmonious sequences which run through all the admirable discoveries of Pasteur give us the sensation of a veritable and gigantic poem?

In Fabre also it seems that the passion which he brings to all his patient observations is in itself truly creative: " his heart beats with emotion, the sweat drips from his brow to the soil, making mortar of the dust "; he forgets food and drink, and " thus passes hours of oblivion in the happiness of learning." I have seen him in his laboratory studying the spawning of the bluebottle, when I, at his side, could scarcely support the horrible stench which rose from the putrefying adders and lumps of meat; he, however, was oblivious of the frightful odour, and his face was inundated with smiles of delight.

Intelligence, then, must here be the servant of feeling and intuition; a kind of primitive faculty, mysterious and instinctive, which alone makes a great naturalist like Fabre, a great historian like Michelet, a great physician like Boherhaave or Bretonneau.

These last are not always the most scholarly nor the most learned nor the most patient, but they are those who possess in a high degree that special vision, that gift, properly speaking poetic,

which is known as the clinical eye, which at
the first glance perceives and confirms the
diagnosis in all its detail.

Fabre has a mind propitious to such processes ;
and if, by chance, circumstances had directed
his attention to medicine, that science which
is based upon an abundant provision of facts,
but in which good sense and a kind of divination play a still wider part, there is no doubt
that he would have been capable of becoming
a shining light in this new arena.

He was full of admiration for that other
illustrious Vauclusian, François Raspail,[16] whose
medical genius anticipated Pasteur and all the
conceptions of modern medicine. It would seem
that he found in him his own temper, his own
fashion of seeing and representing things. He
loved Raspail's books and his prescriptions, full
of reason and a most judicious good sense, dis-
trusting for himself and for his family the complicated formulæ and cunning remedies of an
art too considered and still unproved. At
Carpentras, while his first-born, Émile, was
hovering between life and death, and the
physician who came to see him, " being at
the end of his resources," did nothing more for
him and soon ceased to come, thinking that the

child would not last till the morrow, Fabre flew
to the works of Raspail.

" I searched to discover what his malady was.
I found it, and he was treated day and night
accordingly. To-day he is convalescent; and
his appetite has returned. I believe he is saved,
and I shall say, like Ambroise Paré, ' I have
nursed him; God has cured him.' " [17]

The episode which he relates, when, at the
primary school of Avignon, a retort had just
burst, " spurting in all directions its contents of
vitriol," right in the midst of the suddenly interrupted chemistry lesson, and when, thanks to
his prompt action, he saved the sight of one
of his comrades, does honour to his initiative and
presence of mind.[18]

While " all physicians should bow before the
facts which he excels in discovering," [19] he has
also been able to make direct application of the
marvels of entomology to some of the problems
of hygiene and medicine. He has shown that
the irritant poison secreted by certain caterpillars, " which sets the fingers which handle
them on fire," is nothing but a waste product
of the organism, a derivative of uric acid; he
does not hesitate to perform painful experiments
on himself in order to furnish the proof of his
theory; and he explains thus the curious cases

of dermatitis which are often observed among silkworm-breeders.[20]   He proves the uselessness of our meat-safes of metallic gauze, intended to preserve meat against contamination, and the efficacy of a mere envelope of paper, not only to preserve meat from flies, but also our garments from the clothes-moth.[21]   He recommends the curious Provençal recipe, which consists in boiling suspected mushrooms in salt and water before eating them.   Finally he suggests to members of the medical profession that they might perhaps extract heroic remedies from these treacherous vegetables.[22]

He had need of that indefinite leisure which had hitherto been so wholly lacking, for the events of ephemeral lives occur at indeterminate hours, at unexpected moments, and are of brief duration.

So, attentive to their least movements, Fabre goes forth to observe them at the earliest break of day, in the red dawn, when the bee " pops her head out of her attic window to see what the weather is," and the spiders of the thickets lie in wait under the whorls of their nets, " which the tears of night have changed into chaplets of dewdrops, whose magic jewellery, sparkling in the sun," is already attracting moths and midges.

Seated for hours before a sprig of terebinth, his eye, armed with the magnifying glass, follows the slow manœuvres of the terebinth louse, whose probocis " cunningly distils the venom which causes the leaf to swell and produces those enormous tumours, those misshapen and monstrous galls, in which the young pass their period of slumber."

He watches at night, by the dim light of a lantern, to copy the Scolopendra at her task, seeking to surprise the secret of her eggs ; [23] to observe the Cione constructing her capsule of goldbeater's-skin, or the Processional cater-pillars travelling head to tail along their satin trail, extinguishing his candle only when sleep at last sets his eyelids blinking. He will wake early to witness the fairy-like nocturnal resurrec-tion of the silkworm moth ; [24] " in order not to lose the moment when the nymph bursts her swaddling-bands," or when the wing of the locust issues from its sheath and " commences to sprout " ; no spectacle in the world is more wonderful than the sight of " this extraordinary anatomy in process of formation," the unrolling of these " bundles of tissue, cunningly folded and reduced to the smallest possible compass " in the insignificant alar stumps, which gradually unfold " like an immense set of sails," like the " body-

linen of the princess " of the fairy-tale, which
was contained in one single hemp-seed.[25]

In his Harmas he is like a stranger discovering an unknown world ; " like a kindly
giant from Sirius, holding a magnifying glass
to his eye, retaining his breath, lest it should
overturn and sweep away the pigmies which he
is observing."

His passion for interrogating the Sphinx of
life, everywhere and at all moments, sufficed to
fill his days from one end of the year to the other.
When some distant subject interested him, even
on the most scorching days, he would put " his
lunch in his pocket, an apple and a crust of
bread," and sit out in the hot sunlight, accompanied by his dog, Vasco, Tom, or Rabbit ; fear-
ing only that some importunate third person
might come between nature and himself.

When he walked in his garden he would let
nothing escape him ; witness those precise notes
of an eclipse of the sun, and of the effects which
that phenomenon produces upon animal life as
a whole.

While his children followed the progress of
the moon across the sun through a pane of
smoked glass, he attentively observed all that
occurred in the countryside.

" It is four ; the day grows pale ; the temperature is fresher ; the cocks crow, surprised by this kind of twilight which comes before the hour. A few dogs are baying. . . . The swallows, numerous before, have all disappeared . . . a couple have taken refuge in my study, one window of which is open . . . when the normal light returns they will come outdoors once more. . . . The nightingale, which had so long importuned me by his interminable song, is silent at last ; [26] the black-capped skylarks, which were warbling continually, are suddenly still . . . only the young house-sparrows under the tiles of the roof are mournfully chirping. . . . Peace and silence, the daylight more than half gone. . . . In the Harmas I can no longer see the insects flying ; I find only one bee pillaging the rosemary ; all life has disappeared.

" Only a weevil, the Lixus," which he is observing in a cage, " continues, step by step, without the slightest emotion, his amorous byplay, as though nothing unusual were happening. . . . The nightingale and the skylark may be silent, oppressed by fear ; the bee may re-enter her hive ; but is a weevil to be upset because the sun threatens to go out ? " [27]

He was no less curious concerning the resur-

rection of the sun, and every time he made an
excursion to the Ventoux he was careful not to
miss this spectacle; setting out at an early hour
from the foot of the mountain, so that he might
see the dawn grow bright from the summit of
its rocky mass; then the sun, suddenly rising
in the morning breeze, and setting fire, little by
little, to the Alps of Dauphiné and the hills of
Comtat; and the Rhône, far below, slender as
a silver thread.

He took infinite pleasure too in drinking his
fill of the sublime terrors of the thunderstorm,
which he regarded as one of the most magnificent spectacles which nature can offer; not
content with observing it through glass, he would
open wide the windows at night the better to
enjoy the phosphorescence of the atmosphere,
the conflagration of the clouds, the bursts of
thunder, and all the solemn pomp with which
the great purifying phenomenon manifests itself.

But pure observation, as practised by his
predecessors, Réaumur and Huber, is often insufficient, or "furnishes only a glimpse of
matters."

He had recourse, therefore, to artificial
observation of the kind known as experimentation, and we may say that Fabre was really
the first to employ the experimental method in
the study of the minds of animals.

Near the field of observation, therefore, is the naturalist's workshop, " the animal laboratory," in which such inductions as may be suggested by the doings and the movements of the insects " which roam at liberty amidst the thyme and lavender " are subjected to the test of experiment. It is a great, silent, isolated room, brilliantly lighted by two windows facing south, upon the garden, one at least of which is always kept open that the insects may come and go at liberty.

In the glass-topped boxes of pine which occupy almost the entire height of the white-washed walls are carefully arranged the collections so patiently amassed ; all the entomological fauna of the South of France, and the sea-shells of the Mediterranean ; an abundant wealth also of divers rarities ; numismatical treasures and fragments of pottery and other prehistorical documents, of which the numerous ossuaries in the neighbourhood of Sérignan, scattered here and there upon the hills, contain many, specimens.

At the top, crowning the façade of glass-topped cases like an immense frieze, is the colossal herbarium, the first volumes of which go back to the early youth of their owner ; all the flora, both of the Midi and the North, those of the plains and those of the mountains, and all the algæ of fresh and salt water.

But it must not be supposed that Fabre attaches any great value to these collections, enormous though the sum of labour which they represent. To him they have been a means of education, a means of organizing and arranging his knowledge, and not of satisfying an idle curiosity; not the amusement of one content with the rind of things. In order to identify at first sight such specimens as one encounters and proposes to examine, one must first of all learn to observe and to see thoroughly, and to school the eyes in the colours and forms peculiar to each individual species.

One may fairly complain of Réaumur, for example, that his knowledge was uncertain and incomplete. Too often he leaves his readers undecided as to the nature of the species whose habits he describes. Fabre himself, by dint of criticizing with so much humour the abuse of classifications, has sometimes allowed himself to fall into the same fault.[28] He has taken good care, however, not to neglect the systematic study of species; witness his *Flora of the Vaucluse* and that careful catalogue of the Coleoptera of the neighbourhood of Avignon which he has not disdained to republish.[29] The truth is that " if we do not know their names the knowledge of the things escapes us," 3⁰ and he was profoundly conscious of the truth of this precept of the great Linnæus.

The middle of the room is entirely occupied by a great table of walnut-wood, on which are arranged bottles, test-tubes, and old sardine-boxes, which Fabre employs in order to watch the evolution of a thousand nameless or doubtful eggs, to observe the labours of their larvæ, the creation and the hatching of cocoons, and the little miracles of metamorphosis, " after a germination more wonderful than that of the acorn which makes the oak."

Covers of metallic gauze resting on earthenware saucers full of sand, a few carboys and flower-pots or sweetmeat jars closed with a square of glass ; these serve as observation or experimental cages in which the progress and the actions of " these tiny living machines " can be examined.

Fabre has revealed himself as a physiologist without rival, of a consummate skill in the difficult and delicate art of experimentation ; the art of making the insect speak, of putting questions to it, of forcing it to betray its secrets ; for experiment is " the only method which can throw any light upon the nature of instincts."

His resources being slender and his mind inventive, he has ingeniously supplemented the poverty of his equipment, and has discovered less costly and less complex means of conducting his experiments ; knowing the secret of extracting the sublimest truth from clumsy combinations of " trivial, peasant-made articles."

He has succeeded, in his rustic laboratory, in applying the rigorous rules of investigation and experimentation established by the great biologists. He has therefore been able to establish his beautiful observations in a manner so indisputable that those who come after him and are tempted to study the same things can but arrive at the same results, and derive inspiration from his researches.

To note with care all the details of a phenomenon is the first essential, so that others may afterwards refer to them and profit by them ; the difficult thing is to interpret them, to discover the circumstances, the whys and wherefores, the consequences, and the connecting links.

But a single fact observed by chance at the wayside, and which would not even attract the attention of another, will be instantly luminous to this searching understanding ; it will suggest questions unforeseen, and will evoke, by anticipation, preconceived ideas and sudden flashes of intuition, which will necessitate the test of experiment.

Why, for example, does the Philanthus, that slender wasp, which captures the honey-bee upon the blossoms in order to feed her larvæ ; why, before she carries her prey to her offspring, does she " outrage the dying insect," by squeezing its crop in order to empty it of honey, in which she appears to delight, and does indeed actually delight?

" The bandit greedily takes in her mouth the extended and sugared tongue of the dead insect ; then once more she presses the neck and the thorax, and once more applies the pressure of her abdomen to the honey-sac of the bee. The honey oozes forth and is instantly licked up. Thus the bee is gradually compelled to disgorge the contents of the crop. This atrocious meal lasts often half an hour and longer, until the last trace of honey has disappeared."

The detailed answer is obtained by experiment, which perfectly explains this " odious feast," the excuse for which is simply maternity. The Philanthus knows, instinctively, without having learned it, that honey, which is her ordinary fare, is, by a very singular " inversion," a mortal poison to her larvæ.[31]

As an accomplished physiologist, Fabre conducts all kinds of experiments. Behind the wires
of his cages, he provokes the moving spectacle of
the scorpion at grip with the whole entomological
fauna, in order to test the effects of its terrible
venom upon various species ; and thus he
discovers the strange immunity of larvæ ; the
virus, " the reagent of a transcendent chemistry,
distinguishes the flesh of the larva from that of
the adult ; it is harmless to the former, but
mortal to the latter " ; a fresh proof that " metamorphosis modifies the substance of the organism
to the point of changing its most intimate
properties." [32]

You may judge from this that he knows
through and through the history of the creatures
which form the subjects of his faithful narratives.
He is informed of the smallest events of their
lives. He possesses a calendar of their births ;
he records their chronology and the succession
of generations ; he has noted their methods of
work, examined their diet, and recorded their
meals. He discovers the motives which dictate
their peculiarities of choice ; why the Cerceris,
for instance, among all the victims at its disposal,
never selects anything but the Buprestis and the
weevils. He is familiar too with their tactics of
warfare and their methods of conflict.

His gaze has penetrated even the most hidden dwellings; those in which the Halictus " varnishes her cells and makes the round loaf which is to receive the egg " ; in which, under the cover of cocoons, murderous grubs devour slumbering nymphs ; even the depths of the soil are not hidden from him, for there, thanks to his artifices, he has surprised the astonishing secret of the Minotaur.

He sifts all doubtful stories ; anecdotes, statements of supposed habits ; all that is incoherent, or ill observed, or misinterpreted ; all the *clichés* which the makers of books pass from hand to hand.

In place of repetition he gives us laws, constant facts, fixed rules.

With incomparable skill, he repeats and tests the ancient experiments of Réaumur.

He is not content to show us that Erasmus Darwin is mistaken ; he points out how it is that he has fallen into error.33

He sets himself to decipher the meaning of old tales, skilfully disengaging the little parcel of truth which usually lies beneath a mass of incorrect or even false statements. He criticizes La Fontaine, and questions the statements of Horus Apollo and Pliny. From a mass of undigested knowledge he has created the living science of

entomology, which had received from Réaumur
a first breath of vitality, in such wise that each
individual creature is presented in his work with
its precise expression and the absolute truth of
its character and attitudes ; the inhabitants of
the woods and fields, whether those which feed
upon the crops or those which live in the crevices
of the rocks, or the obscure workers that crawl
upon the earth ; all those which have a secret
to tell or something to teach us ; the Cigale, so
different from the insect of the fable ; and above
all that beetle whose name had hitherto been
encountered arrayed in the most fantastic
legends, the famous *Scarabæus sacer* of the
tombs, which Fabre preferred to place at the
head of his epic as an agreeable prologue,
although the inquiry relative to his amazing
feats belongs chronologically to a comparatively
recent period of his career.

How moderate he is in such suppositions as
he ventures ; how cautious when his persistent
patience has at last struck against " the inaccessible wall of the Unknowable " ! Then, with
admirable frankness, tranquil and sincere, he
simply owns that " he does not know," unlike
so many others, whose uncritical minds are contented with a fragmentary vision, and run so

far ahead of the facts that they can only promote indefinite illusion and error.

One is surprised indeed to remark how few even of the most learned and well-informed of men have a real aptitude for observation, and a highly instructive book might be written concerning the discrepancies and the weak points in our knowledge. If they were subjected to a sufficiently severe test, how threadbare would appear many of those problems which nature and the world present, and which are regarded as resolved !

How long, for instance, was needed to destroy the legend of the cuckoo, incessantly repeated down to the days of Xavier Raspail, and to us so familiar ; to elucidate its history, and to set it in its true light ! 34

It is by means of such data as these that a science is founded, for theories decay, and only well-observed facts remain irrefragable. With stones such as these, which are hewn by the great artisan, the structures of the future will be built, and our own science, perhaps, will one day be refashioned.

For this reason Fabre's books are an education for all those who wish to devote themselves to observation ; a manual of mental discipline, a true " essay upon method," which should be read by every naturalist, and the most interesting, instructive, familiar and delightful course of training that has ever been known.

On the other hand, it is impossible to conceive what labour this delicate work demands; what perseverance Fabre has required painfully to extract one grain of gold; to glean and unite the definite factors, the positive documents, which served as foundations for each of his essays; lucid, limpid, and captivating as the most delightful of fairy-tales. We are charmed, fascinated, and astonished; we see nothing of the groping advance, the checks, and all the toil and the patience demanded. We do not suspect the long waiting, the hesitation, the desperate length of the inquiries. For example, to establish the curious relations which exist between the wasps and the Volucellæ, what long and repeated experiments were needful! His notebooks, in which he records, from day to day, all that he sees, are evidence of this. What watches in the alley of lilacs, year after year, to decipher the mechanism and the mode of construction of the hunting-net of the Epeïra! Some of these histories, like that of the hypermetamorphosis of the Meloë, were only completed as the result of twenty-five years of

assiduous inquiry, while forty years were required
to complete that of the *Scarabæus sacer,* for
his observation of it was always partial ; it is
almost always impossible to divine what one
cannot see from the little that one does see ; and
as a rule one must return to the same point over
and over again in order to fill up lacunæ.

The majority of the insects which Fabre has
studied are solitary, and are only to be encountered singly, scattered over wide areas of
country.   Some live only in determined spots,
and not elsewhere, such as the famous Cerceris,
or the yellow-winged Sphex, of which no trace
is to be found beyond the limits of the
Carpentras countryside.

The proper season must be watched for ; one
must be ready at any moment to profit by a
lucky chance, and resign oneself to interminable
watches at the bottom of a ravine, or keep on
the alert for hours under a fiery sun.   Often the
chance goes by, or the trail followed proves
false ; but the season is over, and one must
wait for the return of another spring.   The trade
of observer in many cases resembles the exhausting labours of the Sisyphus beetle, painfully pushing his pellet up a rough and stony
path ; so that the team halts and staggers at
every moment, the load spills over and rolls

away, and all has to be commenced over again.

We can now cast back, in order to consider at leisure the immortal study which marked the beginning of his fame, with the greater interest and profit in that Fabre has been able, during his retirement, to generalize and extend his discovery.[35]

Let us first of all note how the observation which Dufour had made of the nest of the Cerceris was transformed in his hands, and what developments he was able to evolve therefrom.

Since they have been definitely established by Fabre these curious facts have been well known. They form perhaps the greatest prodigy presented by entomology, that science so full of marvels.

These wasps nourish themselves only on the nectar of flowers; but their larvæ, which they will never behold, must have fresh and succulent flesh still palpitating with life.

The insect digs a tunnel in the soil, in which she places her eggs, and having provisioned the cell with selected game—cricket, spider, caterpillar, or beetle—she finally closes the entrance, which she does not again cross.

Like nearly all insects, the young wasp is

born in the larval state, and from the moment
of its hatching to the end of its growth—that is
to say, for a period of many days—the grub
enclosed in its cell can look for no help from
without.

Here then is a fascinating problem: either
the victims deposited by the mother are dead,
and desiccation or putrefaction attacks them
promptly, or else they are living, as indeed the
larvæ require; but then " what will become of
this fragile creature, which a mere nothing will
destroy, shut in the narrow chamber of the
burrow among vigorous beetles, for weeks on
end working their long spurred legs; or at grips
with a monstrous caterpillar making play with
its flanks and mandibles, rolling and unrolling
its tortuous folds?"

Such is the thrilling mystery of which Fabre
discovered the key.

With inconceivable ingenuity, the victim is
seized and thrown to the ground, and the wasp
plunges her sting, not at random into the body,
which would involve the risk of death, but at
determined points, exactly into the seat of those
invisible nervous ganglions whose mechanism
commands the various movements of the
creature.

Immediately after these subtle wounds the

prey is paralysed throughout its body; its members appear to be disarticulated, "as though all the springs were broken"; the true corpse is not more motionless.

But the wound is not mortal; not only does the insect continue to live, but it has acquired the strange prerogative of being able to live for a very long period without taking any nourishment, thanks precisely to the condition of immobility, in some sort vegetative, which paralysis confers upon it.

When the hour strikes the hungry larva will find its favourite meat served to its liking; and it will attack this defenceless prey with all the circumspection of a refined eater; " with an exquisitely delicate art, nibbling the viscera of its victim little by little, with an infallible method; the less essential parts first of all, and only in the last instance those which are necessary to life. Here then is an incomprehensible spectacle; the spectacle of an animal which, eaten alive, mouthful by mouthful, during nearly a fortnight, is hollowed out, grows less and less, and finally collapses," while retaining to the end its succulence and its freshness.

The fact is that the mother has taken care to deposit her egg "at a point always the same" in the region which her sting has rendered insensible, so that the first mouthfuls are only feebly resented. But as the enemy goes deeper and deeper " it sometimes happens that the cricket, bitten to the quick, attempts to retaliate ; but it only succeeds in opening and closing the pincers of its mandibles on the empty air, or in uselessly waving its antennæ." Vain efforts : " for now the voracious beast has bitten deep into the spot, and can with impunity ransack the entrails." What a slow and horrible agony for the paralysed victim, should some glimmer of consciousness still linger in its puny brain ! What a terrible nightmare for the little field-cricket, suddenly plunged into the den of the Sphex, so far from the sunlit tuft of thyme which sheltered its retreat !

To paralyse without killing, " to deliver the prey to the larvæ inert but living " : that is the end to be attained ; only the method varies according to the species of the hunter and the structure of the prey ; thus the Cerceris, which attacks the coleoptera, and the Scolia, which preys upon the larvæ of the rose-beetle, sting them only once and in a single place, because there is concentrated the mass of the motor ganglions.

The Pompilus, which selects a spider for its victim, no less than the redoubtable Tarantula, knows that its quarry " has two nervous centres which animate respectively the movements of the limbs and those of the terrible fangs; hence the two stabs of the sting." [36]

The Sphex plunges her dagger three times into the breast of the cricket, because she knows, by an intuition that we cannot comprehend, that the locomotor innervation of the cricket is actuated by three nervous centres, which lie wide apart.[37]

Finally, the Ammophila, "the highest manifestation of the logic of instinct, whose profound knowledge leaves us confounded, "stabs the caterpillar in nine places, because the body of the victim with which it feeds its larvæ is a series of rings, set end to end, each of which possesses its little independent nervous centre." [38]

This is not all; the genius of the Sphex is not yet at the end of its foresight. You have doubtless heard of the comatose state into which the wounded fall when, after a fracture of the skull, the brain is compressed by a violent hæmorrhage or a bony splinter. The physiologists imitate this process of nature when they wish, for example, to obtain, in animals under experiment, a state of complete immobility. But did the first surgeon who thought of trepanning the skull in order to exert on the brain, by means of a sponge, a certain degree of compression, ever imagine that an analogous procedure had long been employed in the insect world, and that these clumsy methods were merely child's play beside the astonishing feats of the Unconscious ?

For the stab in the thoracic ganglions, however efficacious, is often insufficient. Although the six limbs are paralysed, although the victim cannot move, its mandibles, " pointed, sharp, serrated, which close like a pair of scissors, still remain a menace to the tyrant ; they might at least, by gripping the surrounding grasses, oppose a more or less effectual resistance to the process of carrying off." So the preceding manœuvres are consummated by a kind of garrotting ; that is, the insect " takes care to compress the brain of its victim, but so as to avoid wounding it ; producing only a stupor, a simple torpor, a passing lethargy." Is not the ingenious observer justified in concluding that " this is alarmingly scientific "?

Between the dry statements of Dufour, which served Fabre as his original theme, and the unaccustomed wealth of this vast physiological poetry, what a distance has been covered !

How far have we outstripped this barren matter, these shapeless sketches! Dufour, another solitary, who retired to his province, in the depth of the Landes, was above all a descriptive anatomist, and he limited himself to an inventory of the nest of a Cerceris.

For him the Buprestes were dead, and their state of preservation was explained simply as a kind of embalming, due to some special action of the venom of the Hymenoptera.

These facts, therefore, were stated as simple curiosities.

Fabre proved that these victims possessed all the attributes of life excepting movement, by provoking contractions in their members under the influence of various stimulants, and by keeping them alive artificially for an indefinite period.

On the other hand, he demonstrated the comparative innocuousness of the venom of these wasps, some of which, like the great Cerceris or the beautiful and formidable Scolia, alarm by their enormous size and their terrifying aspect; so that the conservation of the prey could not be due to any occult quality, to some more or less active antiseptic virtue of the venomous fluid, but simply to the precision of the stab and the miraculous deftness of the " surgeon."

He also pointed out the fact that the sting of the insect is able immediately to dissociate the nervous system of the vegetative life from that of the correlative life, sparing the former, and taking care not to wound the abdomen, which contains the ganglions of the great sympathetic nerve, while it annihilates the latter, which is more or less concentrated along the ventral face of the thoracic region.

He completed this splendid demonstration, not only by provoking under his own eyes the " murderous manœuvres, the intimate and passionate drama," but also by reproducing experimentally all these astonishing phenomena ; expounding their mechanism and their variations with a logic and lucidity, an art and sagacity which raise this marvellous observation, one of the most beautiful known to science, to the height of the most immortal discoveries of physiology. Claude Bernard, in his celebrated experiments, certainly exhibited no greater invention, no truer genius.

VIII

THE MIRACLE OF INSTINCT

The Spirit Bloweth Whither it Listeth

WHAT is this instinct, which guides the insect to such marvellous results? Is it merely a degree of intelligence, or some absolutely different form of activity?

Is it possible, by studying the habits of animals, to discover some of those elementary springs of action whose knowledge would enable us to dive more deeply into our own natures?

Fabre has presented us to his Sphex, the "infallible paralyser." Are we to credit her not only with memory, but also with the faculty of associating ideas, of judgment, and of pursuing a train of reasoning in respect of her astonishingly co-ordinated actions?

Put to the question by the malice of the operator, the "transcendent" anatomist trips over a mere trifle, and the slightest novelty confounds her.

Without the circle of her ordinary habits, what stupidity, "what darkness wraps her round"!

She retreats; she refuses to understand; " she washes her eyes, first passing her hands across her mouth; she assumes a dreamy, meditative air." What can she be pondering? Under what form of thought, illusion, or mirage does the unfamiliar problem which has obtruded itself into her customary life present itself behind those faceted eyes? [1]

How can we tell? We can only attain to knowledge of ourselves by direct intuition. It is only the idea of our ego which enables us to conjecture what is passing in the brains of our fellows. Between the insect and ourselves no understanding is possible, so remote are the analogies between its organization and our own; and we can only form idle hypotheses as to its states of consciousness and the real motive of its actions.

Consider only that unknown and mysterious energy which the insects display in their operations and their labours, as it is in itself, and let us content ourselves, first of all, with comparing it to our own intelligence, such as we conceive it to be.

In seeking to appreciate whereby it differs perhaps we shall gain more than by vainly seeking points of resemblance. We shall discover, in fact, behind the insect and its prodigious instincts, a vast and remote horizon, a region at once more profound, more extensive, and more fruitful than that of the intelligence; and if Fabre is able to help us to decipher a few pages of " the most difficult of all volumes, the book of ourselves," it is precisely, as a philosopher told him, because " man has remained instinctive in process of becoming intelligent." [2]

The work of Fabre is from this point of view an invaluable treasury of observations and experiments, and the richest contribution which has ever been made to the study of these fascinating problems.

" The function of the intelligence is to reflect, to be conscious; that is, to relate the effect to its cause, to add a *because* to a *why;* to remedy the accidental; to adapt a new course of conduct to new circumstances."

In relation to the human intelligence thus defined Fabre has considered these nervous aptitudes, so well adjusted, according to the evolutionists, by ancient habit, that they have finally become impulsive and unconscious, and, properly speaking, innate. He has demonstrated, with an abundance of proof and a power of argument that we must admire, the blind mechanism which determines all the manifestations, even the most extraordinary, of that which we call instinct, and which heredity has fixed in a species of unchangeable automatism, like the rhythm of the heart and the lungs.3

Let us, from this wealth of material, from among the most suggestive examples, select some of his most striking demonstrations, which are classics of their kind.

Fabre has not attempted to define instinct, for it is indefinable ; nor to probe its essential nature, which is impenetrable. But to recognize the order of nature is in itself a sufficiently fascinating study, without striving to crack an unbreakable bone or wasting time in pondering insoluble enigmas. The important matter is to avoid the introduction of illusions, to beware of exceeding the data of observation and experiment, of substituting our own inferences for the facts, of outstripping reality and amplifying the marvellous.

Let us listen to the scrupulous analysis whose lessons, scattered through four thousand pages, teach us more concerning instinct and its innumerable variations than all the most learned treatises and speculations of the philosophers.

Nothing in the world perplexes the mind of

the observer like the spectacle of the birth and growth of the instincts.

At precisely the right moment, just as failure or disaster seems foreordained by the previously established circumstances, Fabre shows us his insects as suddenly mastered by an irresistible force.

" At the right moment " they invincibly obey some sort of mysterious and inflexible prescription. Without apprenticeship, they perform the very actions required, and blindly accomplish their destiny.

Then, the moment having passed, the instincts " disappear and do not reawaken. A few days more or less modify the talents, and what the young insect knew the adult has often forgotten." [4]

Among the Lycosæ, at the moment of exodus, a sudden instinct is evolved which a few hours later disappears never to return. It is the climbing instinct, unknown to the adult spider, and soon forgotten by the emancipated young, who are destined to roam upon the face of the earth. But the young Lycosæ, anxious to leave the maternal home and to travel, become suddenly ardent climbers and aeronauts, each releasing a long, light thread which serves it as parachute. The voyage accomplished, no trace of this ingenuity is left. Suddenly acquired, the climbing instinct no less suddenly disappears.[5]

The great historiographer of instinct has thrown a wonderful light, by his beautiful experiments relating to the nidification of the mason-bee, upon the indissoluble succession of its different phases ; the lineal concatenation, the inevitable and necessary order which presides over each of these nervous discharges of which the total series constitutes, properly speaking, a mode of action.

The mason-bee continues to build upon the ready-completed nest presented to her. She obstinately insists upon provisioning a cell already duly filled with the quantity of honey required by the larva, because, in this case as in the other, the impulse which incites her to build or to provision the nest has not yet been exhausted.

On the other hand, if we empty the little cup of its contents when she has filled it she will not recommence her labours. " The process of provisioning being complete, the secret impulse which urged her to collect her honey is no longer active. The insect therefore ceases to store her honey, and, in spite of this accident, lays her egg in the empty cell, thus leaving the future nursling without nourishment." [6]

In the case of the Pelopæus, Fabre calls our attention to one of the most instructive physiological spectacles that can be imagined.

While the mason-bee does not notice that her cell has been emptied, the Pelopæus cannot perceive that the tricks of the experimenter have resulted in the disappearance of her progeny; and she "continues to store away spiders for a germ that no longer exists; she perseveres untiringly in her useless hunting, as though the future of her larva depended on it; she amasses provisions which will feed no one; more, she pushes aberration to the extent of plastering even the place where her nest was if we remove it, giving the last strokes of the trowel to an imaginary building, and putting her seals upon empty nothing." [7]

From these facts, and others, no less celebrated, which show "the inability of insects to escape from the routine of their customs and their habitual labours," Fabre derives so many proofs of their lack of intelligence.

The *Epeïra fasciata* is incapable of replacing a single radial thread in the geometrical structure of its web, when broken; it recommences the entire web every evening, and weaves it at one stretch with the most beautiful mastery, as though merely amusing itself.

The caterpillar of the Greater Peacock moth teaches us the same lesson; when occupied in weaving its cocoon it does not know how to repair an artificial rent; and " in spite of the certainty of its death, or rather that of the future butterfly, it quietly continues to spin, without troubling to cover the rent; devoting itself to a superfluous task, and ignoring the treacherous breach, which leaves the cocoon and its inhabitant at the mercy of the first thief that finds it." [8]

Thus " because one action has just been performed, another must inevitably be performed to complete the first; what is done is done, and is never repeated. Like the watercourse, which cannot climb the hills and return to its source, the insect does not retrace its steps or repeat its actions, which follow one another invariably, and are inevitably connected in a necessary order, like a series of echoes, one of which awakens another. . . . The insect knows nothing of its marvellous talents, just as the stomach knows nothing of its cunning chemistry. It builds like a bricklayer, weaves, hunts, stabs, and paralyses, as it secretes the venom of its weapons, the silk of its cocoon, the wax of its comb, or the threads of its web; always without the slightest knowledge of the means and the end." [9]

Thus instinct is one thing and intelligence is another ; and for Fabre there is no transition which can transform the one into the other.

But how profound and abundant, how infinite is the source from which this manifold activity derives, distributed as it is throughout the entire animal kingdom ; and which in ourselves commands the profoundest part of our nature ; unconscious, or even in opposition to our wonderful intelligence, which it often silences or altogether overwhelms.

Although the insect " has no need of lessons from its elders " in order to accomplish its beautiful masterpieces, the comprehensive concept of the genius which rises spontaneously and at a single step to the loftiest conceptions is not always a product of pure reason.

Compare the sublime logic of animal maternity, the impeccable dictates of instinct, with the hesitations, the gropings, the uncertainties, the errors and tragic failures of human maternity, when it seeks to replace the unerring commands of instinct by the clumsy efforts of the intelligence !

If all is darkness to the animal, apart from its habitual paths, how feeble and hesitating, how faltering and unequal is reason when it seeks to oppose its laborious inductions to the infallible wisdom of the unconscious !

It is, in fact, to this concatenation of actions, narrowly connected by a mutual dependence, that we owe this inexhaustible series of cunning industries and wonderful arts. To Fabre they are so many feats of a learned unconsciousness.

" See the nest, the accustomed masterpiece of mothers ; it is more often than otherwise an animal fruit, a coffer full of germs, containing eggs in place of seeds."

The satin bag of the *Epeïra fasciata,* in which her eggs are enclosed, " breaks at the caress of the sun, like the skin of an over-ripe pomegranate."

The Dorthesia, the louse inhabiting the euphorbia, " trebles the length of her body, prolonging its hinder part into a pouch, comparable to that of the opossum, into which the eggs are dropped, and in which the young are hatched, to leave it afterwards at will." [10]

The Chermes of the ilex " hardens into a rampart of ebony, whence an innumerable legion of vermin bursts forth one day without changing their place."

The capsule of gold-beater's skin, in which the grubs of the Cione is enclosed, divides itself,

at the moment of liberation, into two hemi-
spheres " of a regularity so perfect that they
recall exactly the bursting of the pyxidium when
the seed is distributed." [11]

Here and there, however, we catch a glimpse
of a rudiment of what we understand by consciousness, in the shape of a " vague discrimina-
tion."

Each plant has its lover, drawn to it by a
kind of elective affinity and invariable tendency.
The Larra makes for the thistle, the Vanessa for
the nettle, the Clytus for the ilex, and the
Crioceris for the lily. " The weevil knows
nothing but its peas and beans, the golden
Rhynchites only the sloe, and the Balaninus only
the nut or acorn."

But the Pieris, which haunts the cabbage,
frequents the nasturtium also, and the golden
rose-beetle, which " intoxicates itself at the
clusters of the hawthorn," is no less addicted to
the nectar of the rose.

The Xylocopa, which burrows in the trunks
of trees and old rafters, forming little round
corridors in which to lodge her offspring, " will
utilize artificial galleries which she has not herself
bored."

The Chalicodoma " also is aware of the

economic advantages of an old abandoned nest " ;
the Anthophora is careful to establish her
family " at the least expense," and profits on
occasion by galleries which have been mined
by previous generations ; adapting herself to
these new conditions, she repairs the tunnels
which she did not construct " and economizes her
forces." [12]

It would seem, therefore, that these tiny minds
are created and shaped by means of experience ;
they recognize " that which is most fitting " ;
they learn, they compare ; may we not also say
that they judge?

Does not the mason-bee, " which rakes the
roads for a dry powdery dust and mixes it with
saliva to convert it into a hard cement," foresee
that this mud will harden?

Is the Pelopæus devoid of judgment when
she seeks the interior of dwelling-houses in order
to shelter her nest of dried clay, which the least
drop of rain would reduce to its original state
of mud?

Is it without knowledge of the effects that the
sloe-weevil builds a ventilating chimney to
prevent the asphyxiation of her larva? that the
Scarabæus sacer contrives a filter at the smaller
end of its pear-shaped ball, by means of which

the grub is able to breathe? or that *Arachne labyrintha* " introduces in her silk-work a rampart of compressed earth to protect her eggs from the probe of the Ichneumon "?

May we not also see a masterpiece of the highest logic in the house of the trap-door spider, *Arachne clotho*, which is furnished with a door, a true door " which she throws open with a push of the leg, and carefully bolts behind her on returning by means of a little silk "? [13]

What a miracle of invention too is the prodigious nest of the Eumenes, " with its egg suspended by a thread from the roof, like a pendulum, oscillating at the lightest breath in order to save it from contact with the caterpillars, which, incompletely paralysed, are wriggling and writhing below " !   Later, when the egg is hatched, " the filament is transformed into a tube, a place of refuge, up which the grub clambers backwards.   At the least sign of danger from the mass of caterpillars the larva retreats into its sheath and ascends to the roof, where the wriggling swarm cannot reach it." [14]

Let us refer also to the remarkable history of the Copris. We cannot deny that the valiant dung-beetle is capable of " evading the accidental " (which to Fabre constitutes one of the distinctive characteristics of the intelligence), since it immediately intervenes if with the point of a penknife we open the roof of its nest and lay bare its egg. " The fragments raised by the knife are immediately brought together and soldered, so that no trace is left of the injury, and all is once more in order." We may read also with what incredible address the mother Copris was able to use and to profit by the ready-made pellets of cow-dung which it occurred to Fabre to offer her.[15]

But their scope is limited, and encroaches very little, in the eyes of the great observer, on the domain of intelligence. This he demonstrates to satiety, and his astonishing Necrophori, which adapt themselves so admirably to circumstances and triumph over the experimental difficulties to which he subjects them, seem scarcely to exceed the limits of those actions which at bottom are merely unconscious.[16]

With the spawning of the Osmia, Fabre throws a fresh and unexpected light on the intuitive knowledge of instinct.

We are still groping our way among the causes which rule the determination of the sexes. Biology has only been able to throw a few scattered lights on the subject, and we possess only a few approximate data ; which nevertheless are turned to account by the breeders of insects. We are still in the region of illusion and imperfect prognostics.

But the Osmia knows what we do not. She is deeply versed in all physiological and anatomical knowledge, and in the faculty of creating children of either sex at will.

These pretty bees, " with coppery skin and fleece of ruddy velvet," which establish their progeny in the hollow of a bramble stump, the cavity of a reed, or the winding staircase of an empty snail-shell, know the fixed and immutable genetic laws which we can only guess at, and are never mistaken.

This marvellous prerogative the Osmia shares with a host of apiaries, in which the unequal development of the males and females requires an unequal provision of space and of nourishment for the future larvæ. For the females, who exceed in point of size, huge cells and abundant provision; for the more puny males, narrow cells and a smaller ration of pollen and honey.

Now the circumstances which are encountered by the Osmia, when, pressed by the necessities of spawning, she searches for a dwelling, are often fortuitous and incapable of modification; and in order to give each set of larvæ the necessary space " she lays at will a male or a female egg, according to the conditions of space."

In this marvellous study, which constitutes, with the history of the Cerceris, the finest masterpiece of experimental entymology, Fabre brilliantly establishes all the details of that curious law which in the Hymenoptera rules both the distribution and the succession of the sexes. In his artificial hives, in glass cylinders, he forces the Osmia to commence her spawning with the males, instead of beginning with the females as nature requires, since the insect is primarily pre-occupied with the more important sex, that which ensures *par excellence* the perpetuation of the species. He even forces the whole swarm which buzzes about his work-tables, his books, his bottles, and apparatus, completely to change the order of its spawning. He shows finally that in the heart of the ovaries the egg of the Osmia has as yet no determined sex, and that it is only at the precise moment when the egg is on the point of emerging from the oviduct that it receives, *at the will of the mother,* the mysterious, final, and inevitable imprint.

But whence does the Osmia derive this " distinct idea of the invisible "? Here again is one of those riddles of nature which Fabre declares himself quite incapable of solving.[17]

Is this all? No; we are far from having

made the tour of this miraculous and incommensurable kingdom through which this admirable
master leads us, and I should never be done
were I to attempt to exhaust all the spectacles
which he offers us. Let us descend yet another
step, among creatures yet smaller and humbler.
We shall find tendencies, impulses, preferences,
efforts, intentions, " Machiavellic ruses and unheard-of stratagems."

Certain miserable black mites, living specks,
the larvæ of a beetle, one of the Meloidæ, the
Sitaris, are parasites of the solitary bee, the
Anthophora. They wait patiently all the winter
at the entrance of her tunnel, on the slope of a
sunny bank, for the springtime emergence of the
young bees, as yet imprisoned in their cells of
clay. A male Anthophora, hatched a little earlier
than the females, appears in the entrance of the
tunnel ; these mites, which are armed with robust
talons, rouse themselves, hasten to and fro, hook
themselves to his fleece, and accompany him in
all his peregrinations ; but they quickly recognize
their error ; for these animated specks are well
aware that the males, occupied all day long in
scouring the country and pillaging the flowers,
live exclusively out of doors, and would in nowise serve their end. But the moment comes
when the Anthophora pays court to the fair

we shall not find a single point in all this physical architecture which will positively inform us of the habits of the insect. Of what account are a few slight differences? It is in the psychical far more than in the anatomical differences that the inviolable demarcation between two species exists. Instincts dominate forms ; the tool does not make the artisan ; " and none of these various structures, however well adapted they may appear to us, bears within it its reason or its finality."

Thus whatever opinion we may hold as to the nature of instinct, the accomplishments and habits of insects are not, properly speaking, connected with the external and visible form of their organs, and their acts do not necessarily presuppose the instruments which would be appropriate to them.

We know that with most organisms, and particularly with plants, an almost imperceptible variation in material circumstances is often enough to modify their character and to produce fresh aptitudes. Nevertheless, we can but wonder, with Fabre, that physical modifications, which, when they do exist, are so slight always as to have escaped the most perfect observation, should have sufficed to determine the appearance of profoundly dissimilar faculties. Inexplicable abilities, unexpected habits, unforeseen physical aptitudes, and unheard-of industries are exercised by means of organs which are here and there practically identical. " The same tools are equally good for any purpose. Talent alone is able to adapt them to manifold ends."

The Anthidia have two particular industries ; " those which felt cotton and card the soft down of hairy plants have the same claws, the same mandibles, composed of the same portions as those which knead resin and mix it with fine gravel." [21]

The sloe-weevil " bores the hard stone of the sloe with the same rostrum as that which its congeners, so like it in conformation, employ to roll the leaves of the vine and the poplar into tiny cigars."

The implement of the Megachile, the rose-fly, is by no means appropriate to its industry ; " yet the perfectly circular fragments of leaves have the precise perfection of form that a punch would give."

The Xylocopa, in order to pierce wood and to bore its galleries in an old rafter, employs " the same utensils which in others are transformed into picks and mattocks to attack clay and gravel, and it is only a predisposition of talent that holds each worker to his speciality."

Moreover, have not the superior animals the same senses and the same structure, yet what inequality there is among them, in the matter of aptitudes and degrees of intelligence !

Habits are no more determined by anatomical peculiarities than are aptitudes or industries.

The two Goat-moth caterpillars, of similar structure, have entirely different stomachic aptitudes ; " the exclusive portion of the one is the oak and of the other the hawthorn or the cherry-laurel."

" Whence does the Mantis derive its excessive hunger, its pugnacity, its cannibalism, and the Empusa its sobriety, its peaceableness, when their almost identical organization would seem to indicate an identity of needs, instincts, and habits ? "

In the same way the black scorpion appears to present none of the interesting peculiarities which we observe in the habits of its congener, the white scorpion of Languedoc.[22]

Structure, therefore, tells us nothing of aptitude ; the organ does not explain its function. Let the specialists hypnotize themselves over their lenses and microscopes ; they may accumulate at leisure masses of details relating to this or that family or genus or individual ; they may undertake the most subtle inquiries, may write thousands and thousands of pages in order to detail a few slight variations, without even succeeding in exhausting the matter : they will not even have seen what is most wonderful.

When the little insect has for the last time cleaned its claws, the secret of the little mind has fled for ever, with all the feelings that animated it and gave it life. That which is crystallized in death cannot explain what was life. This is the thought which the Provençal singer, with that intuition which is the privilege of genius, has expressed in these melodious lines :

> " Oh ! pau de sèn qu'emé l'escaupre
> Furnant la mort, creson de saupre,
> La vertu de l'abiho e lou secrèt doù méu."

> (O men of little sense, who seek,
> Scalpel in hand, to make Death tell
> The virtue of the bee, the secret of her cell !) [23]

IX

EVOLUTION OR "TRANSFORMISM"

" How did a miserable grub acquire its marvellous knowledge? Are its habits, its aptitudes, and its industries the integration of the infinitely little, acquired by successive experiences on the limitless path of time?"

It is in these words that Fabre presents the problem of evolution.

Difficult though it may be to follow the sequence of forms which have endlessly succeeded and replaced one another on the face of the earth, since the beginning of the world, it is certain that all living creatures are closely related ; and the magnificent and fertile hypothesis of evolution, which seeks to explain how extant forms are derived from extinct, has the immense advantage of giving a plausible reason for the majority of the facts which at least cease to be completely unintelligible.

Otherwise we can certainly never imagine how

so many instincts, and these so complex and perfect, could have issued suddenly " from the urn of hazard."

But Fabre will suppose nothing ; he will only record the facts.   Instead of wandering in the region of probabilities, he prefers to confine him-self to the reality, and for the rest to reply simply that " we do not know."

This stern, positive, rigorous, independent, and observant mind, nourished upon geometry and the exact sciences, which has never been able to content itself with approximations and probabilities, could but distrust the seductions of hypotheses.

His robust common sense, which was always his protection against precipitate conclusions, too clearly comprehends the limits of science and the necessity of accumulating facts " upon the thorny path of observation and experiment " to indulge in generalization.   He feels that life has secrets which our minds are powerless to probe, and that " human knowledge will be erased from the archives of the world before we know the last word concerning the smallest fly."

This is why he was regarded as " suspect " by the company of official scientists, to whom he was a dissenter, almost a traitor, especially at a moment when the theories of evolution, then in the first flush of their novelty, were everywhere the cause of a general elation.

No one as yet was capable of divining the man of the future in this modest thinker who would not accept the word of the masters interested, but in opposing the theory of transformation, far from being reactionary, Fabre revealed himself, at least in the domain of animal psychology, as an innovator, a true precursor.

Moreover, his observations, always so direct and personal, often revealed the contrary of what was asserted or foreseen by the magic formulæ suggested by the mind.

To the ingenious mechanism invented by the transformists he preferred to oppose, not contrary argument, but the naked undeniable fact, the obvious testimony, the certain and irrefragable example. " Is it," he would ask them, " to repulse their enemies that certain caterpillars smear themselves with a corrosive product? But the larva of the *Calosoma sycophanta,* which feeds on the Processional caterpillar of the oak-tree, pays no heed to it, neither does the Dermestes, which feeds on the entrails of the Processional caterpillar of the pine-tree."

And consider mimicry. According to the theory of evolution, certain insects would utilize their resemblance to certain others in order to conceal themselves, and to introduce themselves into the dwellings of the latter as parasites living at their expense. Such would be the case with the Volucella, a large fly whose costume, striped with brown and yellow bands, gives it a rude resemblance to the wasp. Obliged, if not for its own sake at least for that of its family, to force itself into the wasp's dwelling as a parasite, it deceitfully dresses itself, we are told, in the livery of its victim, thus affording the most curious and striking example of mimicry; and naturalists insufficiently informed would regard it as one of the greatest triumphs of evolution.

Now what does the Volucella do? It is true that it lays its eggs without being disturbed in the nest of the wasp. But, as the rigorous observer will tell you, it is a precious auxiliary and not an enemy of the community. Its grubs, far from disguising or concealing themselves, " come and go openly upon the combs, although every stranger is immediately massacred and thrown out." Moreover, " they watch the hygiene of the city by clearing the nest of its dead and ridding the larvæ of the wasps of their excretory products." Plunging successively into each chamber of the dormitory the forepart of their bodies, " they provoke the emission of that fluid excrement of which the larvæ, owing to their cloistration, contain an extreme reserve." In a word, the grubs of the Volucella " are the nurses of the larvæ," performing the most intimate duties." [1]

What an astonishing conclusion ! What a disconcerting and unexpected reply to the " theories in vogue " !

Fabre, however, with his poetic temperament and ardent imagination, seemed admirably prepared to grasp all that vast network of relations by which all creatures are connected ; but what proves the solidity of his imperishable work is that all theories, all doctrines, and all systems may resort to it in turn and profit by his proofs and arguments.

And he himself, although he boasts with so much reason of putting forward no pretensions, no theories, no systems, has he not even so yielded somewhat to the suggestions of the prevailing school of thought, and have not his verdicts against evolution often been the more excessive in that he has paid so notable a tribute to the evolutionary progress of creation?

In the first place, he is far from excluding the undeniable influence of environing causes ;

the immense *rôle* of those myriad external
circumstances on which Lamarck so strongly
insisted ; but the work of these factors is, in
his eyes, only accessory and wholly secondary in
the economy of nature ; and in any case it is far
from explaining the definite direction and the
transcendent harmony which characterize evolution, both in its totality and in its most
infinitesimal details.

In one of his admirable little textbooks,
intended to teach and to popularize science, he
complacently enumerates the happy modifications
effected by that " sublime magician," selection,
as understood by Darwin.   He evokes the
metamorphoses of the potato, which, on the
mountains of Chili, is merely a wretched
venomous tubercle, and those of the cabbage,
which on the rocky face of oceanic precipices
is nothing but a weed, " with a tall stem and
scanty disordered leaves of a crude green, an
acrid savour, and a rank smell " ; he speaks
of wheat, formerly a poor unknown grass ; the
primitive pear-tree " an ugly intractable thorny
bush, with detestable bitter fruit " ; the wild
celery, which grows beside ponds, " green all
over, hard, with a repulsive flavour, and which
gradually becomes tenderer, sweeter, whiter,"
and " ceases to distil its poison." [2]

With profound exactitude this great biologist has also perceived the degree to which size may be modified; may dwindle to dwarfness when a niggardly soil refuses to furnish beast and plant alike with a sufficient nourishment.

Without any communication with the other scientists who were occupied by the same questions, knowing nothing of the results which these experimenters had attained in the case of small mammiferous animals, and which prove that dwarfness has often no other cause than physiological poverty, he confirmed and expanded their ideas from an entomological point of view.[3]

Scarcely ever, indeed, was he first inspired by the doings of others in this or that direction; he read scarcely anything, and nature was his sole teacher. He considered that the knowledge to be obtained from books is but so much vapour compared with the realities; he borrowed only from himself, and resorted directly to the facts as nature presented them. One has only to see his scanty library of odd volumes to be convinced how little he owes to others, whether writers or workers.

A true naturalist philosopher, this profound observer has also thrown a light upon certain singular anomalies which, in the insect world, seem to constitute an exception, at all events in our Europe, to the general rules. It is not only to the curiosity and for the amusement of entomologists that he proposes these curious anatomical problems, but also, and chiefly, to the Darwinian wisdom of the evolutionists.

Why, for example, is the *Scarabœus sacer* born and why does it remain maimed all its life; that is to say, deprived of all the digits on the anterior limbs?

" If it is true that every change in the form of an appendage is only the sign of a habit, a special instinct, or a modification in the conditions of life, the theory of evolution should endeavour to account for this mutilation, for these creatures are, like all others, constructed on the same plan and provided with absolutely the same appendages."

The posterior limbs of the *Geotrupes stercorarius*, " perfectly developed in the adult, are atrophied in the larvæ, reduced to mere specks."

The general history of the species, of its migrations and its changes, will doubtless one day throw light upon these strange infirmities, here temporary and there permanent, which may perhaps be explained by unforeseen encounters with undiscovered specimens, strayed perhaps into distant countries.4

What invaluable documents for the entomologist and the historian of the evolution of the species are those multiple and fabulous metamorphoses of the Sitares and the Meloïdæ which this indefatigable inquirer has revealed in all their astonishing phases !

One of the finest examples of scientific investigation is the pursuit, through a period of twenty-five years, with a sagacity which seems to border on divination, of this problem of *hyper-metamorphosis*. The larvæ of those coleoptera which we have seen introduced, with infernal cunning, into the cells of the Anthophora,* suffer no less than four moults before they become nymphs.

These merely external transformations, which involve only the envelope, and respect the internal structure, correspond each with a change of environment and of diet. Each time the organism adapts itself to its new mode of existence, " as perfectly as when it becomes adult " ; and we see the insect, which was clear-sighted, become blind ; it loses its feet, to recover them later ; its slender body becomes ventripotent ; hard, it grows soft ; its mandibles, at first steely, become hollowed out spoonwise, each modification of conformation having its motive in a fresh

* See p. 183.

modification of the conditions of the creature's
life.

How explain this strange evolution of a
fourfold larval existence, these successive appearances of organs, which become entirely unlike
what they were, to serve functions each time
different?

What is the reason, the intention, the high
law which presides over these visible changes,
these successive envelopments of creatures one
within the other, these multiple transfigurations?

By what bygone adaptations has the Sitaris
successively acquired these divers extraordinary
phases of life, indicating possibly for each
corresponding age some ancient and remote
heredity? [5]

How many other arguments might evolution
derive from his books, and what illustrations
of the Darwinian philosophy has he unconsciously furnished!   Does he not even allow
the admission to escape him that "the spirit
of cunning and deception is transmitted"?   He
sees in the persecutions of the Dytiscus, the
"pirate of the ponds," the origin of the faculty
which the Phryganea has of refashioning its
shield when demanded of it.   "To evade the
assault of the brigand, the Phryganea must
hastily abandon its mantle; it allows itself to

sink to the bottom, and promptly removes itself ;
necessity is the mother of invention." [6]

Returning to the lacunæ which it so amazes
Fabre to discover in our organization, even in
the most perfect of us, are they fundamentally
very real? These mysterious and unknown
senses which he has so greatly contributed to
elucidate in the case of the inferior species : why,
he asks, have we not inherited them, if we are
truly the final term and the supreme goal of
creation?

But in cultivating our intuition, as Bergson
invites us to do, would it be impossible to reawaken, deep within us, these strange faculties,
which perhaps are only slumbering? What of
that species of indefinable memory which permits
the red ant, the Bembex, the Cerceris, the Pompilus, the Chalicodoma and so many others to
"find themselves," to orientate themselves with
infallible certainty and incredible accuracy? Is
it not to be found, according to travellers, in
those men who have remained close to nature
and accustomed from their remotest origins to
listen to the silence of the great deserts?

Finally, the evolutionists, who " reconstruct the
world in imagination," and who see in the
relationship of neighbouring species a proof of

descent or derivation, and a whole ideal series, will not fail to perceive throughout his work, in the elementary operations of the Eumenes and the Odynerus, cousins of the Cerceris, which sting their prey in places as yet ill determined, not indeed so many isolated attempts, but an incomplete process of invention, an attempt at procedures still in the fact of formation : in a word, the birth of that marvellous instinct which ends in the transcendent art of the Sphex and the Ammophila.

Although they have acquired such prodigious deftness, these master paralysers are not, in fact, always infallible. Occasionally the Sphex blunders and gropes, " operates clumsily " ; the cricket revives, gets upon its feet, turns round and round, and tries to walk. But, inquires Fabre, do you say that having profited by a fortuitous act, which has turned out to be favourable to them, they have perfected themselves by contact with their elders, " thanks to the imitation of example," and that they have thus crystallized their experiences, which have been transmitted by heredity—thereby fixed in the race ? 7

How much we should prefer that it were so ! How much more comprehensible and interesting their life would become !

But "when the hymenopteron breaks its cocoon, where are its masters? Its predecessors have long ago disappeared. How then can it receive education by example?"

You who "shape the world to your whim," you will reply: "Doubtless there are no longer masters to-day; but go back to the first ages of the globe, when the world in its newness, as Lucretius has so superbly said, as yet knew neither bitter cold nor excessive heat; [8] an eternal springtide bathed the earth, and the insects, not dying, as to-day, at the first touch of frost, two successive generations lived side by side, and the younger generation could profit at leisure by the lessons of example." [9]

Let us return to Fabre's laboratory, to the covers of wire-gauze, and note what becomes, at the approach of winter, of the survivors of the vespine city.

In the mild and comfortable retreat where the wasps are kept under observation they die no less, despite their well-being and all the care expended on them, when once "the inexorable hour" has struck, and once the exact capital of life which seems to have been imparted to them ages ago is exhausted. With no apparent cause, we see death busy among them. "Suddenly the wasps begin to fall as though struck by lightning ; for a few moments the abdomen quivers and the legs gesticulate, then finally remain inert, like a clockwork machine whose spring has run down to the last coil." [10]   This law is general ; " the insect is born orphaned both of mother and father, excepting the social insect, and again excepting the dung-beetle, which dies full of days." [11]

Moreover, Fabre is never weary of demonstrating that the insect, perfectly unconscious of the motive which makes it act, is thereby incapable of profiting by the lessons of experience and of innovation in its habits, beyond a very narrow circle. " No apprentices, no masters." In this world each obeys " the inner voice " on its own account ; each sets itself to accomplish its task, not only without troubling as to what its neighbour is doing, but without thinking any further as to what it is doing itself ; instance the Epeïra, turning its back on its work, yet " the latter proceeds of itself, so well is the mechanism devised " ; and if by ill chance the spider acted otherwise it would probably fail.

Darwin knew barely the tenth part of the colossal work of Fabre. He had read firstly in the *Annals of Natural Science* of the habits of the Cerceris and the fabulous history of the

Meloidæ. Finally he saw the first volume of the *Souvenirs* appear, and was interested in the highest degree by the beautiful study on the sense of location and direction in the mason-bees.

This was already more than enough to excite his curiosity and to make him wonder whether all his philosophy would not stumble over this obstacle.

After having succeeded in explaining so luminously—and with what a lofty purview—the origin of species and the whole concatenation of animal forms, would it not be as though he halted midway in his task were the sanctuary of the origin of instinct to remain for ever inscrutable?

Fabre had not yet left Orange when Darwin engaged in a curious correspondence which lasted until the former had been nearly two years at Sérignan, and which showed how passionately interested the great theorist of evolution was in all the Frenchman's surprising observations.

It seems that on his side Fabre took a singular interest in the discussion on account of the absolute sincerity, the obvious desire to arrive at the truth, and also the ardent interest in his own studies, of which Darwin's letters were full.

He conceived a veritable affection for Darwin, and commenced to learn English, the better to understand him and to reply more precisely ; and a discussion on such a subject between these two great minds, who were, apparently, adversaries, but who had conceived an infinite respect for one another, promised to be prodigiously interesting.

Unhappily death was soon to put an end to it, and when the solitary of Down expired in 1882 the hermit of Sérignan saluted his great shade with real emotion. How many times have I heard him render homage to this illustrious memory !

But the furrow was traced ; thenceforth Fabre never ceased to multiply his pin-pricks in " the vast and luminous balloon of transformism (evolution), in order to empty it and expose it in all its inanity." [12] By no means the least original feature of his work is this passionate and incisive argument, in which, with a remarkable power of dialectic, and at times in a tone of lively banter, he endeavoured to remove " this comfortable pillow from those who have not the courage to inquire into its fundamental nature." He attacked these " adventurous syntheses, these superb and supposedly philosophic deductions," all the more eagerly because he himself had an unshakable faith in the absolute certainty of his own discoveries, and because he asserted the reality of things only after he had observed and re-observed them to satiety.

This is why he cared so little to engage in argument relating to his own works; he did not care for discussion; he was indifferent to the daily press; he avoided criticism and controversy, and never replied to the attacks which were made upon him; he rather took pains to surround himself with silence until the day when he felt that his researches were ripe and ready for publicity.

He wrote to his dear friend Devillario, shortly after Darwin's death:

"I have made a rule of never replying to the remarks, whether favourable or the reverse, which my writings may evoke. I go my own gait, indifferent whether the gallery applauds or hisses. To seek the truth is my only preoccupation. If some are dissatisfied with the result of my observations — if their pet theories are damaged thereby—let them do the work themselves, to see whether the facts tell another story. My problem cannot be solved by polemics; patient study alone can throw a little light on the subject.[13]

"I am profoundly indifferent to what the newspapers may say about me," he wrote to his brother seventeen years later; "it is enough for me if I am pretty well satisfied with my own work." [14]

He read all the letters he received only in a superficial manner, neglecting to thank those who praised or congratulated him, and above all shrinking from all that idle correspondence in which life is wasted without aim or profit.

"I fume and swear when I have to cut into my morning in order to reply to so-and-so who sends me, in print or manuscript, his meed of praise; if I were not careful I should have no time left for far more important work."

His beloved Frédéric, "the best of his friends," was himself often treated no better, and to excuse his silence and the infrequency of his letters, Henri, even in the years spent at Carpentras and Ajaccio, could plead only the same reasons: his stupendous labours, his exhausting task, "which overwhelmed him, and was often too great, not for his courage, but for his time and his strength." [15]

Nevertheless, while evading the question of origins, his far-sighted intellect was bound to "read from the facts" concerning the genesis of new species in process of evolution; and his observations throw a singular light on the quite recent theory of sudden mutations.

The nymph of the Onthophagus presents "a strange paraphernalia of horns and spurs which the organism has produced in a moment of ardour—a luxurious panoply which vanishes in the adult."

The nymph of the Oniticella also decks itself in "a temporary horn, which departs when it emerges."

And "as the dung-beetle is recent in the general chronology of creatures, as it takes rank among the last comers, as the geological strata are mute concerning it, it is possible that these horn-like processes, which always degenerate before they reach completion, may be not a reminiscence but a promise, a gradual elaborations of new organs, timid attempts which the centuries will harden to a complete armour, *and if this were so the present would teach us what the future is to be.*" [16]

Here is a specific transformation, a veritable creation; fortuitous, blind, and silent; one of those innumerable attempts which nature is always making, for the moment a mere matter of hazard, until some propitious circumstance fixes it in future incarnations.

Thus millions of indeterminate creatures are incessantly roughed out in the substance of that microcosm which is the initial cell; and it is here that Fabre sees the real secret of the law of evolution.

He refutes the great principle of Leibnitz, which was so brilliantly adopted by Darwin, that changes occur by degrees, by "fine shades," by slow variations, as the result of successive adaptations, and that there is no jumping-off place in nature. On the contrary, life often passes suddenly from one form to another, by abrupt and capricious leaps, by irregular and disorderly steps, and it is in the egg that Fabre sees the first lineaments of these mysterious and spontaneous variations.

Species are therefore born as a whole, each *at the same time, at the same moment*, "bringing into being its new organism, with its individual properties and peculiarities, its indelible and innate faculties and tendencies, like "so many medals, each struck with a different die, which the gnawing tooth of time attacks only sooner or later to annihilate it."

However, Fabre affirms the continuity of progress; he believes in a better and more merciful future, a more complete humanity, ruled by more harmonious or less brutal laws.

With what profound intelligence and what generous enthusiasm he seeks to conjecture what this future might be, in his beautiful observations on the young of the Lycosa,[17] which can live for weeks and months in absolute abstinence, although we can perceive no reserve of nutriment !

We know no other sources of animal activity save the energy derived from food. Vegetables draw the materials of their nourishment from the soil and the air, and the sunlight is only an intermediary which enables the plant to fix its carbon. The animal species in turn borrow the elements indispensable to their existence from the vegetable world, or restore their flesh and blood with the flesh and blood of other animals.

Now the young Lycosæ "are not inert on their mother's back; if they fall from the maternal chine they quickly pick themselves up and climb up one of her legs, and once back in place they have to preserve the equilibrium of the mass. In reality they know no such thing as complete repose. What then is the energetic aliment which enables the little Lycosæ to struggle? Whence is the heat expended in action derived?"

Fabre sees no other source than "the sun." "Every day, if the sky is clear, the Lycosa, loaded with her little ones, crawls to the edge of her well, and for long hours lies in the sun. There, on the maternal back, the young ones stretch themselves out, saturate themselves in the sunshine, charging themselves with motor reserves, steeping themselves in energy, directly converting into movement the calorific radiations coming from the sun, the centre of all life."

The Scorpion also is able to live for months without nourishment, restoring directly, in the form of movement, "the effluvia emanating from the sun or from other ambient energies—heat, electricity, light — which are the soul of the world."

Perhaps, among the innumerable worlds of space, there is somewhere, gravitating round a fixed star, a planet invisible to us where "the sunlight sates the hunger of the blind."

The gentle philosophy of the ingenious dreamer soothes itself with the vision, entertained by great and noble minds, of a humanity "whose teeth will no longer attack sensible life, nor even the pulp of fruits"; "when creatures will devour one another no longer, will no longer feed upon the dead; when they will be nourished by the sunlight, without conflict, without war, without labour; freed from all care, and assured against all needs !"

Thus, in the humblest creatures, he sees the most marvellous perspectives ; the body of the lowest insect becomes suddenly a transcendent secret, lighting up the abyss of the human soul, or giving it a glimpse of the stars.

And although his work is in contradiction to the theories of the evolutionists, it ends with the same moral conclusion, namely, that all creation moves slowly and without intermission on its gradual ascent towards progress.

X

THE ANIMAL MIND

THE cunning anatomist has now successively laid bare all the springs of the animal intellect; he has shown how the various movements are mutually combined and engaged. But so far we have seen only one of the faces of the little mind of the animal; let us now consider the other aspect, the moral side, the region of feeling, the problem of which is confounded with the problem of instinct, and is doubtless fundamentally only another aspect of the same elemental power.

After the conflict the insect manifests its delight; it seems sometimes to exult in its triumph; " beside the caterpillar which it has just stabbed with its sting, and which lies writhing on the ground," the Ammophila " stamps, gesticulates, beats her wings," capers about, sounding victory in an intoxication of delight.

The sense of property exists in a high degree

among the mason-bees; with them right comes before might, and " the intruder is always finally dislodged." [1]

But can we find in the insect anything analogous to what we term devotion, attachment, affectionate feeling? There are facts which lead us to believe we may.

Let us go once more into Fabre's garden and admire the Thomisus : absorbed in her maternal function, the little spider lying flat on her nest can strive no longer and is wasting away, but persists in living, mere ruin that she is, in order to open the door to her family with one last bite. Feeling under the silken roof her offspring stamping with impatience, but knowing that they have not strength to liberate themselves, she perforates the capsule, making a sort of practicable skylight. This duty accomplished, she quietly surrenders to death, still grappled to her nest.

The Psyche, dominated by a kind of unconscious necessity, protects her nursery by means of her body, anchors herself upon the threshold, and perishes there, devoted to her family even in death.

However, Fabre will show us with infallible logic that all these instances of foresight and maternal tenderness have, as a rule, no other motive than pleasure and the blind impulse which urges the insect to follow only the fatal path of its instincts.

In many species the material fact of maternity is reduced to its simplest expression.

The Pieris limits herself to depositing her eggs on the leaves of a cabbage, " on which the young must themselves find food and shelter."

" From the height of the topmost clusters of the centaury the Clythris negligently lets her eggs fall to the ground, one by one, here or there at hazard; without the least care as to their installation.

" The eggs of the Locustidæ are implanted in the earth like seeds and germinate like grain."

But stop before the Lycosa, that magnificent type of maternal love which Fabre has already depicted. " She broods over her eggs with anxious affection. With the hinder claws resting on the margin of the well she holds herself supported above the opening of the white sac, which is swollen with eggs. For several long weeks she exposes it to the sun during half the day. Gently she turns it about in order to present every side to the vivifying light. The bird, in order to hatch her eggs, covers them with the down of her breast, and presses them against that living calorifer, her heart. The

Lycosa turns hers about beneath the fires of heaven ; she gives them the sun for incubator." [2] Could abnegation be more perfect? What greater proof could there be of renunciation and self-oblivion?

But appearances are vain. Substitute for the beloved sac some other object, and the spider " will turn about, with the same love, as though it were her sac of eggs, a piece of cork, a pincushion, or a ball of paper," just as the hen, another victim of this sublime deception, will give all her heart to hatching the china nesteggs which have been placed beneath her, and for weeks will forget to feed.

The young brood hatches, and the spider goes a-hunting, carrying her little ones on her back ; she protects them in case of danger, but is incapable of recognizing them or of distinguishing them from the young of others. The Copris and the Scorpion are no less blind, " and their maternal tenderness barely exceeds that of the plant, which, a stranger to any sense of affection or morality, none the less exercises the most exquisite care in respect of its seeds."

Moreover, the impulse to work is only a kind of unconscious pleasure. When the Pelopæus " has stored her lair with game," when the Cerceris has sealed the crypt to which she has confided the future of her race, neither one nor the other can foresee " the future offspring which their faceted eyes will never behold, and the very object of their labours is to them occult."

With them, as with all, life can only be a perpetual illusion.

Yet the marvellous edifice of the *Souvenirs entomologiques* is consummated by the astonishing history of the Minotaur, whose habits surpass in ideal beauty all that could be imagined.

At the bottom of a burrow, in a deeply sunken vault, two dung-beetles are at work, the Minotaurs, who, once united, recognize one another, and can find one another again if separated, but do not voluntarily separate, realizing " the moral beauty of the double life " and " the touching concept of the family, the sacred group *par excellence*." The male buries himself with his companion, remains faithful to her, comes to her assistance, and " stores up treasure for the future. Never discouraged by the heavy labour of climbing, leaving to the mother only the more moderate labour, keeping the severest for himself, the heavy task of transport in a narrow tunnel, very deep and almost vertical, he goes foraging, forgetful of himself, heedless of the intoxicating delights of spring, although it would be so good to see something of the country, to feast with his brothers, and to pester the neighbours ; but no ! he collects the food which is to nourish his children, and then, when all is ready for the new-comers, when their living is assured, having spent himself without counting the cost, exhausted by his efforts, and feeling himself failing, he leaves his home and goes away to die, that he may not pollute the dwelling with a corpse."

The mother, on her side, allows nothing to divert her from her household, and only returns to the surface when accompanied by her young, who disperse at will. Then, having nothing more to do, the devoted creature perishes in turn.3

Compared with the Scarabæus, which contents itself with idle wandering, or even with the meritorious Sisyphus, does it not seem that the Minotaur moves on an infinitely higher plane?

What nobler could be found among ourselves? What father ever better comprehended his duties and obligations toward his family? What morality could be more irreproachable ; what fairer example could be meditated?

" Is not life everywhere the same, in the body of the dung-beetle as in that of man? If we examine it in the insect, do we not examine it in ourselves? "

Whence does the Minotaur derive these particular graces?   How has it risen to so high
a level on the wings of pure instinct?   How
could we explain the rarity of so sublime an
example, did we not know, to satiety, that
" nature everywhere is but an enigmatic poem,
as who should say a veiled and misty picture,
shining with an infinite variety of deceptive
lights in order to evoke our conjectures "? [4]

Nevertheless, it is a fact that the majority,
have no other rule of conduct than to follow
the trend of their instincts, and to obey " their
unbridled desires."   No one better than Fabre
has expounded the blind operation of these little
natural forces, the brutality, of their manners,
their cannibalism, and what we might call their
amorality, were it possible to employ our human
formulæ outside our own human world.

With the gardener-beetles, if one is crippled,
none of the same race halts or lingers ; none
attempts to come to his aid.   Sometimes the
passers-by hasten to the invalid to devour him."

In the republic of the wasps " the grubs recog-
nized as incurable are pitilessly torn from their
place and dragged out of the nest.   Woe to
the sick ! they are helpless and at once expelled."

When the winter comes all the larvæ are

massacred, and the whole vespine city ends in a horrible tragedy.

But life is a whole, and all conduct is good whose actions realize an object and are adapted to an end. If there is a " spirit " of the hive, the insect also has its morality and the wasp's nest its " law," and the conduct of its inmates, horrible though it may seem to Fabre, is doubtless only a submission to certain exigencies of that universal law which makes nature a " savage foster-mother who knows nothing of pity."

These cruelties particularly show us that one of the functions of the insect in nature is to preside over the disappearance and also the ultimate metamorphoses of the least " remnants of life."

Each has its providential hygienic function.

The Necrophori, " the first of the tiny scavengers of the fields," bury corpses in order to establish their progeny in them ; in the space of a few hours an enormous body, a mole, a water-rat, or an adder, will completely disappear, buried under the earth.

The Onthophagi purify the soil, " dividing all filth into tiny crumbs, ridding the earth of its defilements."

A very small beetle, the Trox, has the im-prescriptible mission of purging the earth of the rabbits' fur rejected by the fox.5

Here structure explains the function.

The intestine of the grub of the rose-beetle " is a veritable triturating mill, which transforms vegetable matter into mould ; in a month it will digest a volume of matter equal to several thousand times the initial volume of the grub."

The intestine of the Scarabæi is prolonged to a prodigious length in order to " drain the excre-ment to the last atom in its manifold circuits. The sheep has finely divided the vegetable matter ; the grub, that incomparable triturator, reduces it to the finest possible consistency ; not a morsel is left in which the magnifying glass can reveal a fibre."

To fulfil its hygienic mission the insect arrives in due season, and multiplies its legions ; " there are twenty thousand eggs in the flanks of the house fly ; immediately they are hatched these twenty thousand maggots set to work, so that Linnæus has said that three flies would suffice to devour the body of a horse or a lion."

Feeding only upon wheat, a single weevil, the Calendar beetle, produces ten thousand eggs, whence issue as many larvæ, each of them devouring its grain.

In all species the number of births is at first exaggerated, for all, the obscure, the nameless, the most destructive, our pests as well as our most precious helpers, have their utility and their part to play in the general scheme of life, a *raison d'être* in the eternal renewal of things, which is without reference to the vexatious or beneficent quality of their behaviour to us.

Each has its rank assigned, each has its task, to one the flower, to another the roots, to a third the leaves ; the vine has its caterpillars, its beetles, its butterflies ; the clover, its moths and mites.[6]

Man sees himself forced to submit to them, and spends himself in vain efforts to carry on an often useless campaign. Nothing seems to affect them, neither drought, nor rain, nor even the severest cold ; and the eggs and larvæ, organizations apparently delicate in the extreme, are often more tenacious of life than the adults. Fabre has proved this : let the temperature suddenly fall twenty degrees : the eggs of Geotrupes and the larvæ of the cockchafer or the rose-beetle endure such vicissitudes of temperature with impunity ; contracted and stiffened into little masses of ice, but not destroyed, they revive in spring no less than the eel fry, the rotifers, or the tardigrades. One can scarcely believe that life still persists in a state of suspense only in these little frozen creatures, whose organization is already so complicated.

Then, of a sudden, the ravagers disappear; more often than not none knows how or why; deliverance is at hand. What indeed would become of the world were nothing to moderate such fecundity?

Again, each species has its trials which appear in time to moderate its surplusage, and Fabre expounds for us, with a stern philosophy, the terrible devices by which this repression is effected.

Each has its appointed enemy, which lives upon it or its offspring, and which in turn becomes the prey of some smaller creature. The gentle itself, " the king of the dead," has its parasites. While it swims in the deliquescence of putrefying flesh a minute Chalcidian perforates its skin with an imperceptible wound, and introduces its terrible eggs, whence in the future will issue larvæ which to-morrow will devour the devourers of to-day.

None exists save to the detriment of others. Everywhere, even in the smallest, we find " an atrocious activity, a cunning brigandage," a

savage extermination, which dominates a vast
unconscious world of which the final result is
the restoration of equilibrium.7   It is only on
these antagonisms, on the enemies of our
enemies, that we can found any hope of
seeing this or that pest disappear.   A small
Hymenopteron, almost invisible, the *Microgaster
glomeratus,* is entrusted with the destruction of
the cabbage caterpillar ; the cochineal wages war
to the death upon the green-fly ; the Ammophila is the predestined murderer of the harvest
Noctuela, whose misdeeds in a beetroot country
often amount to a disaster.   The Odynerus has
for its instinctive mission to arrest the excessive
multiplication of a lucerne weevil, no less than
twenty-four of whose grubs are necessary to
rear the offspring of the brigand, and nearly
sixty gadflies are sacrificed to the growth of a
single Bembex.

Everywhere craft is organized to triumph over
force. Around each nest the parasites lie in wait,
" atrocious assassins of the child in the cradle,
watching at the doors for the favourable occasion to establish their family at the expense of
others.   The enemy penetrates the most inaccessible fortress ; each has its tactics of war,
devised with a terrible art.   Of the nest and

the cocoon of the victim the intruder makes its own nest, its own cocoon, and in the following year, instead of the master of the house, he will emerge from underground as the usurping bandit, the devourer of the inhabitant."

While the cicada is absorbed in laying her eggs an insignificant fly labours to destroy them. How express the calm audacity of this pigmy, following closely after the colossus, step by step ; several at once almost under the talons of the giant, which could crush them merely by treading on them? But the cicada respects them, or they would long ago have disappeared." [8]

Fabre thus agrees with Pasteur, who in the world of the infinitely little shows us the same antagonisms, the same vital competition, the same eternal movement of flux and reflux, the same whirlpool of life, which is extinguished only to reappear : tending always towards an equilibrium which is incessantly destroyed. And it is thanks to this balancing that the integral of life remains everywhere and always almost identical with itself.

XI

HARMONIES AND DISCORDS

SUCH indeed is the economy of nature that secret relations and astonishing concordances exist throughout the whole vast weft of things. There are no loose ends; everything is consequent and ordered. Hidden harmonies meet and mingle.

Among the terebinth lice, " when the population is mature, the gall is ripe also, so fully do the calendars of the shrub and the animal coincide "; and the mortal enemy of the Halictus, the sinister midge of the springtime, is hatched at the very moment when the bee begins to wander in search of a location for its burrows.

The fantastic history of the larvæ of the Anthrax furnishes us with one of the most suggestive examples of these strange coincidences.[1]

The Anthrax is a black fly, which sows its eggs on the surface of the nests of the mason-bee, whose larvæ are at the moment reposing in their silken cocoons.

" The grub of the Anthrax emerges and comes to life under the touch of the sunlight. Its cradle is the rugged surface of the cell; it is welcomed into the world by a literally stony harshness. . . . Obstinately it probes the chinks and pores of the nest; glides over it, crawls forward, returns, and recommences. The radicle of the germinating seed is not more persevering, not more determined to descend into the cool damp earth. What inspiration impels it? What compass guides it? What does the root know of the fertility of the soil? . . . The nursling, the seed of the Anthrax, is barely visible, almost escaping the gaze of the magnifying glass; a mere atom compared to the monstrous foster-mother which it will drain to the very skin. Its mouth is a sucker, with neither fangs nor jaws, incapable of producing the smallest wound; it sucks in place of eating, and its attack is a kiss." It practises, in short, a most astonishing art, " another variation of the marvellous art of feeding on the victim without killing it until the end of the meal, in order always to have a store of fresh meat. During the fourteen days through which the nourishment of the Anthrax continues, the aspect of the larva remains that of living flesh; until all its substance has been literally transferred, by a kind of transpiration, to the body of the nursling, and the victim, slowly exhausted, drained to the last drop, while retaining to the end just enough life to prove refractory to decomposition, is reduced to the mere skin, which, being insufflated, puffs itself out and resumes the precise form of the larva, there being nowhere a point of escape for the compressed air."

Now the grub of the Anthrax " appears precisely at the exact moment when the larva of the Chalicodoma is attacked by that lethargy which precedes metamorphosis, and which renders it insensible, and during which the substance of the grub about to be transfigured into a bee commences to break down and resolve itself into a liquid pulp, for the processes of life always liquefy the grub before achieving the perfect insect." [2]

Here again the time-tables coincide.

But it is perhaps in the celebrated Odyssey of the grub of the Sitaris that Fabre most urgently claims our admiration for the marvellous and incomprehensible wisdom of the Unconscious !

Let us recapitulate the unheard-of series of events, the inextricable complication of circumstances, which are required to condition the lowly life of a Sitaris.

In the first place, this microscopic creature must be provided with talons, or how could it adhere to the fleece of the Anthophora, on which it must live as parasite for a certain length of time?

Then again, it must transfer itself from the male to the female bee in the course of its travels abroad, or its destiny would be cut short.

Again, it must not miss the opportunity of embarking itself upon the egg just at the propitious moment.

Then the volume of this egg must be so calculated as to represent an allowance of food exactly proportioned to the duration of the first phase of its metamorphosis. Moreover, the quantity of honey accumulated by the bee must suffice for the whole of the remaining cycle of its larval existence.

Let a single link of the chain be broken, and the entire species of the Sitaris is no longer possible.

If every species has its law; if the Geotrupes remain faithful to filth, although experience shows that they can accommodate themselves equally well to the putrefaction of decayed leaves; if the predatory species—the Cerceris, the Sphex, the Ammophila—resort only to one species of quarry to nourish their larvæ, although these same larvæ accept all indifferently, it is on account of those superior economic laws and secret alliances the profound reasons for which as a rule escape us or are beyond the scope of our theories.

For all things are produced and interlocked by the eternal necessity; link engages in link, and life is only a plexus of solitary forces allied among themselves by their very nature, the condition of which is harmony. And the whole system of living creatures appears to us, through the work of the great naturalist, as an immense organism, a sort of vast physiological apparatus, of which all the parts are mutually interdependent, and as narrowly controlled as all the cells of the human body.

Fabre goes on to present us with other facts, which at a first glance appear highly immoral; I am referring to certain phases of sexual love among the lower animals, and his ghoulish revelations concerning the horrible bridals of the Arachnoids, the Millepoda, and the Locustidæ.

The Decticus surrenders only to a single exploit of love; a victim of its " strange genesics "; utterly exhausted by the first embrace, empty, drained, extenuated, motionless in all its members, utterly worn out, it quickly succumbs, a mere broken simulacrum, like the miserable lover of a monstrous succubus who " loves him enough to devour him." [3]

The female scorpion devours the male ; " all is gone but the tail ! "

The female Spider delights in the flesh of her lover.

The cricket also devours a small portion of her " debonair " admirer.

The Ephippigera " excavates the stomach of her companion and eats him."

But the horror of these nuptial tragedies is surpassed by the insatiable lust, the monstrous conjunction, the bestial delights of the Mantis, that " ferocious spectre, never wearied of embraces, munching the brains of its spouse at the very moment of surrendering her flanks to him." [4]

Whence these strange discords, these frightful appetites?

Fabre refers us to the remotest ages, to the depths of the geological night, and does not hesitate to regard these cruelties as " remnants of atavism," the lingering furies of an ancient strain, and he ventures a profound and plausible explanation.

The Locusts, the Crickets, and the Scolo-

pendræ are the last representatives of a very
ancient world, of an extinct fauna, of an early
creation, whose perverse and unbridled instincts
were given free vent, when creation was as yet
but dimly outlined, " still making the earliest
essays of its organizing forces " ; when the
primitive Orthoptera, " the obscure forbears of
those of to-day, were " sowing the wild oats of
a frantic rut," in the colossal forests of the
secondary period ; by the borders of the vast
lakes, full of crocodiles, and antediluvian
marshes, which in Provence were shaded by
palms, and strange ferns, and giant Lycopodia,
never as yet enlivened by the song of a bird.

These monstrosities, in which life was making
its essays, were subject to singular physical
necessities. The female reigned alone ; the male
did not as yet exist, or was tolerated only for
the sake of his indispensable assistance. But
he served also another and less obvious end ;
his substance, or at least some portion of his
substance, was an almost necessary ingredient
in the act of generation, something in the nature
of a necessary excitant of the ovaries, " a horrible
titbit," which completed and consummated the
great task of fecundation. Such, in Fabre's eyes,
was the imperious physiological reason of these

rude laws. This is why the love of the males is almost equivalent to their suicide ; the Gardener-beetle, attacked by the female, attempts to flee, but does not defend himself ; " it is as though an invincible repugnance prevents him from repulsing or from eating the eater." In the same way the male scorpion " allows himself to be devoured by his companion without ever attempting to employ his sting," and the lover of the Mantis " allows himself to be nibbled to pieces without any revolt on his part."

A strange morality, but not more strange than the organic peculiarities which are its foundation ; a strange world, but perhaps some distant sun may light others like it.

These terrible creatures are a source of dismay to Fabre. If all things proceed from an underlying Reason, if the divine harmony of things testifies everywhere to a sovereign Logic, how shall the proofs of its excellence and its sovereign wisdom be found in such things as these?

Far from attributing to the order of the universe a supposed perfection, far from considering nature as the most immediate expression of the Good and the Beautiful, in the words of Tolstoy,5 he sees in it only a rough sketch which a hidden God, hidden, but close at hand, and living eternally present in the heart of His creatures, is seeking to test and to shape.

Living always with his eyes upon some secret of the marvels of God, whom he sees in every bush, in every tree, "although He is veiled from our imperfect senses," [6] the vilest insect reveals to him, in the least of its actions, a fragment of this universal Intelligence.

What marvels indeed when seen from above ! But consider the Reverse—what antinomies, what flagrant contradictions ! What poor and sordid means ! And Fabre is astonished, in spite of all his candid faith, that the fatality of the belly should have entered into the Divine plan, and the necessity of all those atrocious acts in which the Unconscious delights. Could not God ensure the preservation of life by less violent means? Why these subterranean dramas, these slow assassinations? Why has Evil, *the poison of the Good*,[7] crept in everywhere, even to the origin of life, like an eternal Parasite?

Within this fatal circle, in which the devourer and the devoured, the exploiter and the exploited, lead an eternal dance, can we not perceive a ray of light?

For what is it that we see?

The victims are not merely the predestined victims of their persecutors. They seek neither

to struggle nor to escape nor to evade the inevitable ; one might say that by a kind of
renunciation they offer themselves up whole as
a sacrifice !

What irresistible destiny impels the bee to
meet half-way the Philanthus, its terrible enemy?
The Tarantula, which could so easily withstand
the Pompilus, when the latter rashly carries war
into its lair, does not disturb itself, and never
dreams of using its poisoned fangs. Not less
absolute is the submission of the grasshopper
before the Mantis, which itself has its tyrant, the
Tachytes.

Similarly those which have reason to fear for
their offspring, if not for themselves, do nothing
to evade the enemy which watches for them ; the
Megachile, although it could easily destroy it,
is indifferent to the presence of a miserable
midge, " the bandit who is always there, medi-
tating its crime " ; the Bembex, confronted with
the Tachinarius, cannot control its terror, but
nevertheless resigns itself, while squeaking with
fright.

If each creature is what it is only because
it is a necessary part of the plan of the supreme
Artisan who has constructed the universe, why
have some the right of life and death and others
the terrible duty of immolation?

Do not both obey, not the gloomy law of carnage, but a kind of sovereign and exquisite sacrifice, some sort of unconscious idea of submission to a superior and collective interest?

This hypothesis, which was one day suggested to Fabre by a friend of great intellectual culture,[8] charmed and interested him keenly. I noticed that he was more than usually attentive, and he seemed to me to be suddenly reassured and appeased. For him it was as though a faint ray of light had suddenly fallen among these impenetrable and distressing problems.

It seemed to him that by setting before our eyes the spectacle of so many woes, universally distributed, and doubtless necessary, woes which do not spare even the humblest of creatures, the Sovereign Intelligence intends to exhort us to examine ourselves truly and to dispose us to greater love and pity and resignation.

All his work is highly and essentially religious ; and while he has given us a taste for nature, has he not also endeavoured to give us, according to the expression of Bossuet " the taste for God," or at least a sense of the divine? In opposing the doctrine of evolution, which reduces the animal world to the mere virtualities of the cell ; in revealing to us all these marvels which seem destined always to escape human compre-

hension ; finally, by referring us more necessarily
than ever to the unfathomable problem of our
origins, Fabre has reopened the door of mystery,
the door of the divine Unknown, in which the
religion of men must always renew itself.   We
should belittle his thought, we should dwarf the
man himself, were we to seek to confine to any
particular thesis his spiritualistic conception of
the universe.

Fabre recognizes and adores in nature only
the great eternal Power, whose imprint is everywhere revealed by the phenomena of matter.

For this reason he has all his life remained
free from all superstition and has been completely
indifferent to dogmas and miracles, which to his
mind imply not only a profound ignorance of
science, but also a gross and complete miscom-
prehension of the divine Intelligence. He kneels
upon the ground or among the grasses only the
more closely to adore that force, the source of
all order, the intuitive knowledge of which,
innate in all creatures, even in the tiny immov-
able minds of animals, is merely a magnificent
and gratuitous gift. The office in which he
eagerly communicates is that glorious and formidable Mass in which the ragged sower, " noble
in his tatters, a pontiff in shabby small-clothes,
solemn as a God, blesses the soil, more majestic

than the bishop in his glory at Easter-tide." 9
It is there that he finds his " Ideal," in the
incense of the perfumes " which are softly
exhaled from the shapely flowers, from their
censers of gold," in the heart of all creatures,
" chaffinch and siskin, skylark and goldfinch,
tiny choristers " piping and trilling, " elaborating
their motets " to the glory of Him who gave them
voice and wings on the fifth day of Genesis. He
fraternizes with all, with his dogs and his cats,
his tame tortoise, and even the " slimy and
swollen frog "; the " Philosopher " of the
Harmas, whose murky eyes he loves to interrogate as he paces his garden " by the light of
the stars "; persuaded that all are accomplishing
a useful work, and that all creatures, from the
humblest insect which has only nibbled a leaf,
or displaced a few grains of sand, to man
himself, are anointed with the same chrism of
immortality.

And as he has always set the pleasures of
study before all others, he can imagine no
greater recompense after death than to obtain
from heaven permission still to continue in their
midst, during eternity, his life of labour and
effort.

XII

THE INTERPRETATION OF NATURE

WE have noted the essential features of his precise and unfailing vision and the value of the documents which record the work of Fabre, but the writer merits no less attention than the observer and the philosopher.

In the domain of things positive, it is not always sufficient to gather the facts, to record them, and to codify in bare formulæ the results of inquiry. Doubtless every essential discovery is able to stand by itself ; in what would an inventor profit, for example, by raising himself to the level of the artist ? " For the theorem lucidity suffices ; truth issues naked from the bottom of a well."

But the manner of speaking, describing, and depicting is none the less an integral part of the truth when it is a matter of expounding and transmitting the latter. To express it feebly is often to compromise it, to diminish it, and even to betray it. There are terms which say better than others what has to be said. " Words have their physiognomy ; if there are lifeless words, there are also picturesque and richly-coloured words, comparable to the brush strokes which scatter flecks of light on the grey background of the picture." There are particular terms of expression, felicities which present things in a better light, and the writer must search in his memory, his imagination, and his heart, for the fitting accent ; for the flexibility of language and the wealth of words which are needful if he would fully succeed in the portrayal of living creatures ; if he would tender the living truth, reproduce in all its light and shade the spectacle of the world, arouse the imagination, and faithfully interpret the mysterious spirit which impregnates matter and is reflected in thought.

The artist then comes forward to co-ordinate all these scattered fragments, to assemble them, to breathe vitality into them, to restore these inert truths to life.

But what a strange manner of working was Fabre's ; what a curious method of composition ! However full of ideas his mind might be, he was incapable of expressing them if he remained in one place and assumed the ordinary preliminary

attitude of a man preparing to write. Seated
and motionless, his limbs at rest, pen in hand,
with a blank page before him, it seemed to him
that all his faculties became of a sudden paralysed. He must first move about ; activity
helped him to pursue his ideas ; it was in action
that he recovered his ardour and uncovered
the sources of inspiration. Just as he never
observed without enthusiasm, so he found it impossible to write without exaltation, and it was
precisely because he so ardently loved the truth
that he felt himself compelled to show it in all
its beauty.

Moving like a circus-horse about the great
table of his laboratory, he would begin to tramp
indefatigably round and round, so that his steps
have worn in the tiles of the floor an ineffaceable
record of the concentric track in which they
moved incessantly for thirty years.

His mind would grow clear and active as he
walked, smoking his pipe and " using his
marrow-bones." [1] He was already at work ; he
was " hammering " his future chapters in his
brain ; for the idea would be all the more precise
as the form was more finished and more irreproachable, more closely identified with the
thought ; he would wait until the word quivered,
palpitated, and lived ; until the transcription was

no longer an illusion, a phantom, a vision devoid
of reality, but a faithful echo, a sincere trans-
lation, a finished interpretation, reflecting entire
the fundamental essence of the thing ; in a word,
a work of art, a parallel to nature.

Then only would he sit before the little walnut-
wood table " spotted with ink and scarred with
knife-cuts, just big enough to hold the inkstand,
a halfpenny bottle, and his open notebook " :
that same little table at which, in other days,
by force of meditation, he achieved his first
degrees.

Then he would begin to write, " his pen dipped
not in ink only " but in his heart's blood ; [2] first
of all in ordinary ruled notebooks bound in
black cloth, in which he noted, day by day, hour
by hour, the observations of every moment, the
results of his experiments, together with his
thoughts and reflections.   Little by little those
documents would come together which eluci-
dated and completed one another, and at last
the book was written.   These notebooks, these
copious records, are remarkable for the regularity of the writing and the often impeccable
finish of the first draught.   Although here and
there the same data are transcribed several times
in succession, and each time struck through with
a vigorous stroke of the pen, there are whole

pages, and many pages together, without a single erasure. The handwriting, excessively small—one might think it had been traced by the feet of a fly—becomes in later years so minute that one almost needs a magnifying glass to decipher it.

These notebooks are not the final manuscript. The entomologist would write a new and more perfect copy on loose sheets of paper, making one draught after another, patiently fashioning his style and polishing his work, although many passages were included without revision as they were written in the first instance.

The greatest magician of modern letters, versed in all the artifices of the French language, speaking one day of Fabre and his writings, made in my hearing the assertion that he was not, properly speaking, an artist. He might well be a great naturalist, a veteran of science, an observer of genius, but he was by no means and would never be a writer according to the canons of the craft.

But how many others, like him, in their time regarded as " pitiable in respect of their language," charm us to-day, simply because they were gifted with imagination and the power of giving life to their work ! 3

To tell the truth, Fabre is absolutely careless of all literary procedure, and solely preoccupied with bringing his style into harmony with his thoughts; he is not in the least a manufacturer of literary phrases. There is no trace of artistic writing in his books, and it is only his manner of feeling and of expressing himself that makes him so dear to us.

What touches us in him is the accent, the simplicity, the measure, the good sense, and the perfect equilibrium of each of these pages: simple, often commonplace, even incorrect or trivial, but so alive, so human, that the blood seems to flow in them. It is the lover in Fabre that draws us to him; nothing quite like his work has been seen since the days of Jean de La Fontaine.

He has liberated science; he laughs at the specialists who take refuge behind their "barbarian terminologies," at the "jargon" of those "who see the world only through the wrong end of the glass"; at the exaggerated importance which they attribute to insignificant details, the narrowness of classifications, and the chaos of systems; all that incoherent, remote, and inaccessible science, which he, on the contrary, strives to render pleasant and attractive.

This is why the great scientist has endeavoured to speak like other people, preferring, to the harsh consonants of technical phrases which sound " like insults " or have the air of " a magical invocation, which make certain scientific works read like so much gibberish," the " naive and picturesque appellation, the familiar, trivial name, the popular, living term which directly interprets the exact signification of the habits of an insect, or informs us fully of its dominant characteristic, or which, at least, leaves nothing to conjecture."

He considers it useless and even inconvenient to abandon many charming expressions, appropriate and significant as they are, which may be borrowed from the good old French tongue ; and in this he resembles the immortal de Jussieu, who in his botanical classifications was careful not to discard the old popular denominations which Theophrastus, Virgil, and Linnæus had thought fit to bestow upon plant and tree.

It is for the same reasons that he loves the Provençal tongue ; that beautiful idiom, that superb language, rich in music, in sonorous words, so suggestive and so full of colour, many of whose terms, saying precisely what they intend to say, have no equivalent in French.   He has

learned the language, and reads it : in particular
Roumanille, whose easy, familiar style pleases
him better than the grandiloquence of Mistral,
although he delights also in Calendal, whose
lyrical powers fill him with enthusiasm. From
this ancient tongue, which was early as familiar
to him as the French, he borrowed certain
mannerisms, certain tricks of style, certain
neologisms, and also, to some extent, his
simplicity of manner and the cadence of his
prose.

It was not without difficulty that he attained
this mastery. Measure the gulf between his
first volumes and his last ; in the first the style
is slightly nerveless and indefinite : it was only
as he gradually advanced in his career that he
acquired what may be called his final manner,
or achieved, in his narratives, a perfect literary
style. The most substantially constructed, the
most happily expressed of his pages were written
principally in his extreme old age. Not only
is there no sign of failing in these, but in his
latest *Souvenirs* the perfection of form is
perhaps even more remarkable than the wealth
of matter.

How vitally his scrupulous records impress the

mind's eye ; how firmly they establish themselves
in the memory !

Even if one has never seen the Pelopæus, one
readily conceives an impression of " her wasp-
like costume, and curving abdomen, suspended
at the end of a long thread." What exactitude
in this snapshot, taken at the moment when the
insect is occupied in scooping out of the mire
the lump of mud intented for the construction
of her nest : " like a skilled housekeeper, with
her clothing carefully tucked up that it may
not be soiled, the wings vibrating, the limbs
rigidly straightened, the black abdomen well
raised on the end of its yellow stalk, she rakes
the mud with the points of her mandibles,
skimming the shining surface." [4]

He draws, in passing, this charming sketch of
the gadfly, the pest of horses, which nourishes
itself with their blood :

" Gadflies of several species used to take
refuge under the silken dome of my umbrella,
and there they would quietly rest, one here, one
there, on the tightly stretched fabric ; I rarely
lacked their company when the heat was over-
powering. To while away the hours of waiting,
I used to love to watch their great golden eyes,
which would shine like carbuncles on the vaulted
ceiling of my shelter ; I used to love to watch

them slowly change their stations, when the
excessive heat of some point of the ceiling would
force them to move a little." [5]

We follow all the manœuvres of the Balaninus,
the acorn-weevil, " burying her drill " which
" operates by means of little bites." The
narrator calls our attention to the slightest
episodes, even to those accidents which sometimes
surprise the worker in the course of her labours ;
when, with the rostrum buried deep in the acorn,
her feet suddenly lose their hold. Then the
unhappy creature, unable to free herself, finds
herself suspended in the air, at right angles to
her proboscis, far from any foothold or point
of vantage, at the extremity of her disproportionately long pike, that " fatal stake." [6]

As for the poplar-weevil, we can almost see
it moving " in the subtlest equilibrium, clinging
with its hooked talons to the slippery surface
of the leaf " ; we watch all the details of its
methods and the progress of its labours. We
see the flexed leaf assume the vertical under
the awl-stroke which the insect applies to the
pedicle, " when, partially deprived of sap, the leaf
becomes more flexible, more malleable ; it is
in a sense partly paralysed, only half alive."
Then we follow the rolling process ; " the imper-
turbable deliberation of the worker as it rolls

its cigar, which finally hangs perpendicularly at the end of the bent and wounded stem." [7]

Fabre, like a true artist, finds all sorts of expressions to describe the tiny, fragile eggs of his insects ; little shining pearls, delicious coffers of nickel or amber, miniature pots of translucid alabaster, "which we might think were stolen from the cupboard of a fairy."

He opens the enchanted alcoves wherein the puny grubs lie slumbering, "fat, rounded puppets " ; the tender larvæ which " gape and swing their heads to and fro " when the mother returns to the nest with her toothsome mouthful or her crop swollen with honey.

What compassion, what tenderness, what sensitiveness in the affecting picture of the mother Halictus, abandoned, deprived of her offspring, bewildered and lost, when the terrible spring fly has destroyed her house : bald, emaciated, shabby, careworn, already dogged by the small grey lizard ! [8]

The tragedy of the wasps' nest at the approach of the first chills of winter is the final fragment of an epic. At first there is a sort of uneasiness, "a species of indifference and anxiety which broods over the city " ; already it has a presentiment of coming misfortune, of an approaching catastrophe. Presently a wild excitement ensues; the foster-mothers, "frightened, fierce, and restless," as though suddenly attacked by an incomprehensible insanity, conceive an aversion for the young; "the neuters extirpate the larvæ and drag them out of the nest," and the drama of destruction draws to a close with "the final catastrophe; the infirm and the dying are dismembered, eviscerated, dissected in a heap in the catacombs by maggots, woodlice, and centipedes." Finally the moth comes upon the scene, its larvæ "attacking the dwelling itself; gnawing and destroying the joists and rafters, until all is reduced to a few pinches of dust and shreds of grey paper." 9

What picturesque expressions he employs to depict, by means of some significant feature, the striking peculiarities of the insect physiognomy!

"The gipsy who night and day for seven months goes to and fro with her brats upon her back" is the Lycosa, the Tarantula with the black stomach, the great spider of the wastes.

The larva of the great Capricornis, which gnaws the interior of old oak-trees, "leaving behind it, in the form of dry-rot, the refuse of its digestive processes," is "a scrap of intestine which eats its way as it goes."

In "that hideous lout" the Scorpion he shows us a rough epitome of the shapeless head, the truncated face of the spider.

The Tachinæ, those "brazen diptera" which swarm on the sunny sand on the watch for Bembex or Philanthus, in order to establish their offspring at its expense, "are bandits clad in fustian, the head wrapped in a red handkerchief, awaiting the hour of attack!"

The Languedocian Sphex, sprawling flat upon the vine leaves, grows dizzy with the heat and frisks for very pleasure; "with its feet it taps rapidly on its resting-place, and thus produces a drumming like that of a shower of rain falling thickly on the leaves." Fabre takes a keen delight in the production of these pictures, at once so exact and lifelike; but we must not therefore suppose that his mind is incapable of the detailed descriptions necessitated by the laborious processes of minute anatomy.

Like all sciences, entymology has its uninteresting aspects when we seek to study it deeply. Yet with what interest and lucidity has Fabre succeeded in expounding the complex morphoses of the obscure and miserable larva of the Sitaris, the curious intestine of the Scarabæus, the secret of the spawning of the weevil, and the ingenious mechanisms of the musical instruments of the Decticus and the Cicada. With what subtle art he explains the song of the cricket, how the five hundred prisms of the serrated bow set the four tympana in vibration ; and how the song is sometimes muffled by a process of muting.[10]

Some of the images suggested to him by the forms of animals are so beautiful that certain of his descriptions might well serve to inspire an artist, or suggest new motives of decoration in the arts of enamelling, gem-engraving, jewellery, etc.

Instead of eternally copying ancient things, or seeking inspiration in lifeless texts, why not turn our attention to the numerous and interesting motives which are scattered all around us, whose originality consists precisely in the fact that they have never yet been employed? Why torture the mind to produce more painful elaborations of awkward, frozen, poverty-stricken combinations, when Nature herself is at hand, offering the inexhaustible casket of her living marvels, full of the profoundest logic and as yet unexamined?

If the bee by means of the hexagonal prism has anticipated all the geometers in the problem of the economy of space and matter ; if the Epeïra and the mollusc have invented the logarithmic spiral and its transcendent pro- perties ; if all creatures " inspired by an æsthetic which nothing escapes, achieve the beautiful,"[11] surely human art, which can but imitate and remember, has only to employ to its profit and transfigure into ideal images the natural beauties so profusely furnished by the Uncon- scious.

Modern art, influenced more especially by the subtle Japanese, is already treading this path.

What artist could ever engrave on rare metals or model in precious substances a more beauti- ful subject than the wonderful picture of the Tarantula offering, at the length of her extended limbs, her white sac of eggs to the sun ; or the transparent nymph of the *Onthophagus taurus,* " as though carved from a block of crystal, with its wide snout and its enormous horns like those of the Aurochs "? [12]   What an undiscovered subject he might find in the nymph of the Ergatus,[13] with its almost incorporeal grace, as though made of " translucent ivory, like a communicant in her white veils, the arms crossed upon the breast ; a living symbol of mystic resignation before the accomplishment of destiny " ; or in the still more mysterious nymph of the *Scarabœus sacer,* first of all " a mummy of translucent amber, maintained by its linen cerements in a hieratic pose ; but soon upon this background of topaz, the head, the legs, and the thorax change to a sombre red, while the rest of the body remains white, and the nymph is slowly transfigured, assuming that majestic costume which combines the red of the cardinal's mantle with the whiteness of the sacerdotal alb."

On the other hand, what Sims or Bateman ever imagined weirder caricature than the grotesque larva of the Oniticella, with its extravagant dorsal hump ; or the fantastic and alarming silhouette of the Empusa, with its scaly belly raised crozierwise and mounted on four long stilts, its pointed face, turned-up moustaches, great prominent eyes, and a " stupendous mitre " : the most grotesque, the most fantastic freaks that creation can ever have evolved ? [14]

XIII

THE EPIC OF ANIMAL LIFE

ALTHOUGH in his portraits and descriptions Fabre is simple and exact, and so full of natural geniality; although he can so handle his words as to render them " adequate " to reproduce the moving pictures of the tiny creatures he observes, his style touches a higher level, flashes with colour, and grows rich with imagery when he seeks to interpret the feelings which animate them : their loves, their battles, their cunning schemes, and the pursuit of their prey ; all that vast drama which everywhere accompanies the travail of creation.

It is here in particular that Fabre shows us what horizons, as yet almost unexplored, what profound and inexhaustible resources science is able to offer poetry.

The breaking of egg or chrysalid is in itself a moving event ; for to attain to the light is for all these creatures " a prodigious travail."

The hour of spring has sounded. At the call of the field-cricket, the herald of the spring, the germs that slumber in nymph or chrysalis have broken through their spell.

What haste and ingenuity are required to emerge from the natal darkness, to unwrap the swaddling-bands, to break the subterranean shells, to demolish the waxen bulkheads, to perforate the soil or to escape from prisons of silk !

The woodland bug, whose egg is a master-piece, invents I know not what magical centre-bit, what curious piece of locksmith's work, in order to unlock its natal casket and achieve its liberty.

For days the grasshopper " butts its head against the roughness of the soil, and wars upon the pebbles ; by dint of frantic wriggling it escapes from the womb of the earth, bursts its old coat, and is transfigured, opening its eyes to the light, and leaping for the first time."

The Bombyx of the pine-tree " decks its brow with points of diamond, spreads its wings, and erects its plumes, and shakes out its fleece to fly only in the darkness, to wed the same night, and to die on the morrow."

What marvellous inventions, what machinery,

what incredible contrivances, " in order that a tiny fly can emerge from under ground " !

The Anthrax assumes a panoply of trepans, an assortment of gimlets and knives, harpoons and grapnels, in order to perforate its ceiling of cement ; then the lugubrious black fly appears, all moist as yet with the humours of the laboratory of life, steadies itself upon its trembling legs, dries its wings, quits its suit of armour, and takes flight."

The blue-fly, buried in the depth of the sand, " cracks its barrel-shaped coffin," and splits its mask, in order to disinter itself ; the head divides into two halves, between which we see emerging and disappearing by turns a monstrous tumour, which comes and goes, swells and shrivels, palpitates, labours, lunges, and retires, thus compressing and gradually undermining the sand, until at last the newborn fly emerges from the depth of the catacombs.[1]

Certain young spiders, in order to emancipate themselves, to conquer space, and disperse themselves about the world, resort to an ingenious system of aviation. They gain the highest point of the thicket, and release a thread, which, seized by the wind, carries them away suspended. Each shines like a point of light against the foliage of the cypresses. There is a continuous stream of tiny passengers, leaping and descending in scattered sheaves under the caresses of the sun, like atomic projectiles, like the fountain of fire at a pyrotechnic display. What a glorious departure, what an entry into the world ! Gripping its aëronautic thread, the insect ascends in apotheosis ! [2]

But if all are called all are not chosen. " How many can move only at the greatest peril under the rugged earth, proceeding from shock to shock, in the harsh womb of universal life, and, arrested by a grain of sand, succumb half-way " !

There are others whom slower metamorphoses condemn to vegetate still longer in the subterranean night, before they are permitted to assume their festival attire, and share in their turn in the gladness of creation.

Thus the Cicada is forced to labour for long gloomy years in the darkness before it can emerge from the soil. At the moment when it issues from the earth the larva, soiled with mire, " resembles a sewer-man ; its eyes are whitish, nebulous, squinting, blind." Then " it clings to some twig, it splits down the back, rejects its discarded skin, drier than horny parchment, and becomes the Cigale, which is at first of a pale grass-green hue." Then,

> " Half drunken with her joy, she feasts
> In a hail of fire " ;

and all day long drinks of the sugared sap of tender bark, and is silent only at night, sated with light and heat. The song, which forms part of the majestic symphony of the harvest-tide, announces merely its delight in existence. Having passed years underground, the cigale has only a month to reign, to be happy in a world of light, under the caressing sun. Judge whether the wild little cymbals can ever be loud enough " to celebrate such felicity, so well earned and so ephemeral " ! 3

All sing for happiness, each after its kind, through the calm of the summer days. Their minds are intoxicated ; it is their fashion of praying, of adoring, of expressing " the joys of life : a full crop and the sun on the back." Even the humble grasshopper rubs its flanks to express its joy, raises and lowers its shanks till its wing-cases squeak, and is enchanted with its own music, which it commences or terminates suddenly " according to the alternations of sun and shade." Each insect has its rhythm, strident or barely perceptible ; the music of the thickets and fallows caressed by the sun, rising and falling in waves of joyful life.

The insects make merry ; they hold uproarious festival ; and they mate insatiably ; even before forming a mutual acquaintance; in a furious rush of living, for " love is the sole joy of the animal," and " to love is to die."

Hardly unwrapped, still dusty from the strenuous labour of deliverance, " the female of the Scolia is seized by the male, who does not even give her time to wash her eyes." Having slept over a year underground, the Sitares, barely rid of their mummy-cases, taste, in the sunlight, a few minutes of love, on the very site of their re-birth ; then they die. Life surges, burns, flares, sparkles, rushes " in a perpetual tide," a brief radiance between two nights.

A world of a myriad fairies fills the rustling forest : day and night it unfolds a thousand marvellous pictures ; about the root of a bramble, in the shadow of an old wall, on a slope of loose soil, or in the dense thickets.

" The insect is transfigured for the nuptial ceremony ; and each hopes, in its ritual, to declare its passion." Fabre had some thought of writing the Golden Book of their bridals and their wedding festivals ; 4 the Kamasutra of their feasts and rules of love ; and with what art, at once frank and reserved, has he here and there handled this wonderful theme ! In the radiant garden of delight, where no detail of truth is omitted, but where nothing shocks us, Fabre reveals himself as he is in his conversation; evading the subject where it takes a licentious turn; fundamentally chaste and extremely reserved.

At the foot of the rocks the Psyche " appears in the balcony of her boudoir, in the rays of the caressing sun; lying on the cloudy softness of an incomparable eider-down." She awaits the visit of the spouse, " the gentle Bombyx," who, for the ceremony, " has donned his feathery plumes and his mantle of black velvet." " If he is late in coming, the female grows impatient; then she herself makes the advances, and sets forth in search of her mate."

Drawn by the same voluptuous and overwhelming force, the cricket ventures to leave his burrow. Adorned " in his fairest attire, black jacket, more beauteous than satin, with a stripe of carmine on the thigh," he wanders through the wild herbage, " by the discreet glimmer of twilight," until he reaches the distant lodging of the beloved. There at last he arrives " upon the sanded walk, the court of honour that precedes the entry." But already the place is occupied by another aspirant. Then the two rivals fall upon one another, biting one another's heads, " until it ends by the retreat of the weaker, whom the victor insults by a *bravura* cry." The happy champion bridles, assuming a proud air, as of one who knows himself a handsome fellow, before the fair one, who feigns to hide herself behind her tuft of aphyllantus, all covered with azure flowers. " With a gesture of a fore-limb he passes one of his antennæ through his mandibles as though to curl it ; with his long-spurred, red-striped legs he shuffles with impatience ; he kicks the empty air ; but emotion renders him mute." 5

In the foliage of the ash-tree the lover of the female Cantharis thrashes his companion, who makes herself as small as she can, hiding her head in her bosom ; he bangs her with his fists, buffets her with his abdomen, " subjects her to an erotic storm, a rain of blows " ; then, with his arms crossed, he remains a moment motionless and trembling ; finally, seizing both antennæ of the desired one, he forces her to raise her head " like a cavalier proudly seated on horse and holding the reins in his hands."

The Osmiæ " reply by a click of the jaws to the advances of their lovers, who recoil, and then, doubtless to make themselves more valiant, they also execute a ferocious mandibular grimace. With this byplay of the jaws and their menacing gestures of the head in the empty air the lovers have the air of intending to eat one another." Thus they preface their bridals by displays of gallantry, recalling the ancient betrothal customs of which Rabelais speaks; the pretenders were cuffed and derided and threatened with a hearty pummelling.[6]

On the arid hillsides, where the doubtful rays of the moon pierce the storm-clouds and illumine the sultry atmosphere, the pale scorpions, with short-sighted eyes, hideous monsters with mis-shapen heads, " display their strange faces, and two by two, hand in hand, stalk in measured paces amid the tufts of lavender. How tell their joys, their ecstasies, that no human language can express. . . . ! "[7]

However, the glow-worm, to guide the lover, lights its beacon " like a spark fallen from the full moon "; but " presently the light grows feebler, and fades to a discreet nightlight, while all around the host of nocturnal creatures, de-layed in their affairs, murmur the general epithalamium."[8]

But their happy time is soon over; tragedy is about to follow idyll.

One must live, and " the intestine rules the world."

All creatures that fill the world are incessantly conflicting, and one lives only at the cost of another.

On the other hand, in order that the coming generations may see the light, the present generations must think of the preservation of the young. " Perish all the rest provided the brood flourish ! " And in the depth of burrows the future larvæ who live only for their stomachs, " little ogres, greedy of living flesh," must have their prey.

To hunger and maternity let us also add love, which " rules the world by conflict."

Such are the components of the " struggle for existence," such as Fabre has described it, but with no other motive than to describe what he has observed and seen. Such are the ordinary themes of the grandiose battles which he has scattered through his narratives, and never did circus or arena offer more thrilling spectacles ; no jungle ever hid more moving combats in its thickets."

" Each has its ruses of war, its methods of attack, its methods of killing."

What tactics—" studied, scientific, worthy of the athletes of the ancient palæstra "—are those which the Sphex employs to paralyse the Cricket and the Cerceris to capture the Cleona, to secure them in a suitable place, so as to operate on them more surely and at leisure !

Beside these master paralysers, so expert in the art of dealing slow death, there are those which, with a precision no less scholarly, kill and wither their victims at a single stroke, and without leaving a trace: " true practitioners in crime."

On the rock-rose bushes, with their great pink flowers, " the pretty Thomisus, the little crab-spider, clad in satin," watches for the domestic bee, and suddenly kills it, seizing the back of the head, while the Philanthus, also seizing it by the head, plunges its sting under the chin, neither too high nor too low, but " exactly in the narrow joint of the neck," for both insects know that in this limited spot, in which is concentrated a small nervous mass, something like a brain, is " the weak point, most vulnerable of all," the fault in the cuirass, the vital centre.   Others, like the Araneidæ, intoxicate their prey, and their subtle bite, " which resembles a kiss," in whatever part of the body it is applied, " produces almost immediately a gradual swoon."

Thus the great hairy Bourdon, in the course of its peregrinations across the wastes of thyme, sometimes foolishly strays into the lair of the Tarantula, whose eyes glimmer like jewels at the back of his den. Hardly has the insect disappeared underground than a sort of shrill rattling is heard, a " true death-song," immediately followed by the completest silence. " Only a moment, and the unfortunate creature is absolutely dead, proboscis outstretched and limbs relaxed. The bite of the rattlesnake would not produce a more sudden paralysis."

The terrible spider " crouching on the battlements of his castle, his heavy belly in the sun, attentive to the slightest rustling, leaps upon whatever passes, fly or Libellula, and with a single stroke strangles his victim, and drains its body, drinking the warm blood."

To dislodge him from his keep needs all the cunning strategy of the Pompilus ; a terrible duel, a hand-to-hand combat, stupendous, truly epic, in which the subtle address and the ingenious audacity of the winged insect eventually triumph over the dreadful spider and his poisoned fangs." 9

On the pink heather " the timid spider of the thickets suspends by ethereal cables the branching whorl of his snare, which the tears of the night have turned into chaplets of jewels. . . . The magical jewellery sparkles in the sun, attracting mosquitoes and butterflies ; but whosoever approaches too closely perishes, a victim of curiosity." Above the funnel is the trap, " a chaos of springs, a forest of cordage ; like the rigging of a ship dismembered by the tempest. The desperate creature struggles in the shrouds of the rigging, then falls into the gloomy slaughter-house where the spider lurks ready to bleed his prey."

Death is everywhere.

Each crevice of bark, each shadow of a leaf, conceals a hunter armed with a deadly weapon, all his senses on the alert. Everywhere are teeth, fangs, talons, stings, pincers, and scythes.

Leaping in the long grasses, the Decticus with the ivory face " crunches the heads of grass-hoppers in his mandibles."

A ferocious creature, the grub of the Hemero-bius, disembowels plant-lice, making of their skins a battle-dress, covering its back with the eviscerated victims, " as the Red Indian ties about his loins the tresses of his scalped enemies."

Caterpillars are surrounded by the implacable voracity of the Carabidæ :

" The furry skins are gaping with wounds ; their contents escape in knots of entrails, bright green with their aliment, the needles of the pine-tree ; the caterpillars writhe, struggling with loop-like movements, gripping the sand with

their feet, dribbling and gnashing their mandibles. Those as yet unwounded are digging
desperately in the attempt to escape underground.
Not one succeeds. They are scarcely half buried
before some beetle runs to them and destroys
them by an eviscerating wound."

At the centre of its net, which seems " woven
of moonbeams," in the midst of its snare, a
glutinous trap of infernal ingenuity, or hidden at
a distance in its cabin of green leaves, the *Epeïra
fasciata* waits and watches for its prey. Let the
terrible hornet, or the *Libellula auripennis,* flying
from stem to stem, fall into the limed snare ; the
insect struggles, endeavours to unwind itself ;
the net trembles violently as though it would be
torn from its cables. Immediately the spider
darts forward, running boldly to the intruder.
With rapid gestures the two hinder limbs weave a
winding-sheet of silk as they rotate the victim
in order to enshroud it. . . . The ancient Ret-
iarius, condemned to meet a powerful beast of
prey, appeared in the arena with a net of cordage
lying upon his left shoulder ; the animal sprang
upon him ; the man, with a sudden throw, caught
it in the meshes ; a stroke of the trident
despatched it. Similarly the Epeïra throws its
web, and when there is no longer any movement
under the white shroud the spider draws closer ;

its venomous fangs perform the office of the trident.[10]

The Praying Mantis, that demoniac creature which alone among the insects turns its head to gaze, "whose pious airs conceal the most atrocious habits," remains on the watch, motionless, for hours at a time. Let a great grasshopper chance to come by : the Mantis follows it with its glance, glides between the leaves, and suddenly rises up before it ; " and then assumes its spectral pose, which terrifies and fascinates the prey ; the wing-covers open, the wings spring to their full width, forming a vast pyramid which dominates the back ; a sort of swishing sound is heard, like the hiss of a startled adder ; the murderous fore-limbs open to their full extent, forming a cross with the body, and exhibiting the axillæ ornamented with eyes vaguely resembling those of the peacock's tail, part of the panoply of war, concealed upon ordinary occasions. These are only exhibited when the creature makes itself terrible and superb for battle. Then the two grappling-hooks are thrown ; the fangs strike, the double scythes close together and hold the victim as in a vice." [11]

There is no peace ; night falls and the horrible conflict continues in the darkness. Atrocious struggles, merciless duels, fill the summer nights. On the stems of the long grasses, beside the furrows, the glow-worm " anæthetizes the snail," instilling into it its venom, which stupefies and produces sleep, in order to immobilize its prey before devouring it.

Having chorused their joy all the day long in the sunshine, in the evening the Cicadæ fall asleep among the olives and the lofty plane-trees. But suddenly there is a sound as of a cry of anguish, short and strident; it is the despairing lamentation of the cicada, surprised in repose by the green grasshopper, that ardent hunter of the night, which leaps upon the cicada, seizes it by the flank, and devours the contents of the stomach. After the orgy of music comes night and assassination.

Such is the gloomy epic which goes forward among the flowers, amidst the foliage, under the shadowy boughs, and on the dusty fallows. Such are the sights that nature offers amid the profound peace of the fields, behind the flowering of the sudden spring-tide and the splendours of the summer. These murders, these assassinations are committed in a mute and silent world, but " the ear of the mind " seems to hear

> " A tiger's rage and cries as of a lion
> Roaring remotely through this pigmy world."

Was it to these thrilling revelations that Victor Hugo intended to apply these so wonderfully appropriate lines? Was it he who bestowed upon Fabre, according to a poetic tradition, the name of " the Homer of the insects," which fits him so marvellously well?

It is possible, although Fabre himself can cite no evidence to support these suggestions; but let us respect the legend, simply because it is charming, and because it adds an exact and picturesque touch to the portrait of Fabre.

In this drama of a myriad scenes, in which the little actors in their rustic stage play each in his turn their parts at the mercy of occasion, and the hazard of encounter, the humblest creatures are personages of importance.

Like the human comedy, this also has its characters privileged by birth, clothed in purple, dazzling with embroidery, " adorned with lofty plumes," who strut pretentiously; " its idle rich," covered with robes of gold of rustling splendour, who display their diamonds, their topazes and their sapphires; who gleam with fire and shine like mirrors, magnificent of mien; but their brains are " dense, heavy, inept, without imagination, without ingenuity, deprived of all common sense, knowing no other anxiety than to drink in the sunlight at the heart of a rose or to sleep off their draughts in the shadow of a leaf.

Those who labour, on the contrary, do not attract the eye, and the most obscure are often the most interesting. Necessitous poverty has educated and formed them, has excited in them " feats of invention," unsuspected talents, original industries ; a thousand curious and unexpected callings, and no subject of poetry equals in interest the detailed history of one of these tiny creatures, by which we pass without observing them, amid the stones, the brambles, and the dead leaves. It is these above all that add an original and epic note to the vast symphony of the world.

But death also has its poetry. Its shadowy domains hold lessons no less magnificent, and the most putrid carrion is to Fabre a " tabernacle " in which a divine comedy is enacted.

The ant, that " ardent filibuster, comes first, and commences to dissect it piecemeal."

The Necrophori " exhaling the odour of musk, and bearing red pompons at the end of their antennæ," are " transcendent alchemists."

The Sarcophagi, or grey flesh flies, " with red bloodshot eyes, and the stony gaze of a knacker " ; the Saprinidæ, " with bodies of polished ebony like pearls of jet " ; the *Silpha aplata,* with large and sombre wing-cases in mourning; the shiny slow-trotting Horn-beetle; the Dermestes, " powdered with snow beneath the stomach "; the slender Staphylinus; the whole fauna of the corpse, the whole horde of artisans of death, " intoxicating themselves with purulence, probing, excavating, mangling, dissecting, transmuting, and stamping out infection."

Fabre gives a curious exposition of " that strange art " by which the grub of the grey bot-fly, the vulgar maggot, by means of a subtle pepsine, disintegrates and liquefies solid matter; and it is because this singular solvent has no effect upon the epidermis that the fly, in its wisdom, chooses by preference the mucous membranes, the corner of the eye, the entrance of the nostrils, the borders of the lips, the live flesh of wounds, there to deposit its eggs.

With what penetration this original mind has analysed " the operation of the crucible in which all things are fused that they may recommence " and has expounded the marvellous lesson which is revealed by decomposition and putridity !

XIV

PARALLEL LIVES

WE have now seen what entomology becomes in the hands of the admirable Fabre. The vast poem of creation has never had a more familiar and luminous interpreter, and you will nowhere find other work like his.

How far he outstrips Buffon and his descriptions of animals—so general, so vague, so impersonal—his records unreliable and his entire erudition of a second-hand quality!

It is with Réaumur that we are first of all tempted to compare him; and some have chosen to see in him only one who has continued Réaumur's work. In reality he has eagerly read Réaumur, although at heart he does not really enjoy his writings; he has drunk from this fruitful source, but he owes him no part of his own rich harvest.

But there are many affinities between them; they have many traits in common, despite the points of difference between them.

The illustrious son of Rochelle was born, like

Fabre, with a love of all natural things, and before attacking the myriad problems of physics and natural history, wherein he was to shine by so many curious discoveries, he also had prepared himself by a profound study of mathematics.

Luckier than Fabre, however, Réaumur enjoyed not only the advantages of birth, but all the material conditions necessary to his ardent intellectual activity. Fortune overwhelmed her favourite with gifts, and played no small part in his glory by enabling him, from an early age, to profit by his leisure and to give a free rein to his ruling passions. He was no less modest than the sage of Sérignan; self-effacing before others, says one of his biographers, so that they were never made to feel his superiority.[1]

In the midst of the beautiful and spacious gardens at the end of the Faubourg Saint-Antoine, where he finally made his home, he also contrived to create for himself a Harmas after his own heart.

It was there that in the as yet virgin domain of entomology he unravelled the riddle of the marvellous republic of the bees, and was able to expound and interpret a large number of those tiny lives which every one had hitherto despised, and which indeed they continued to despise until the days of Fabre, or at least regarded as absolutely unimportant. He was the first to venture to suspect their connection with much " that most nearly concerns us," or to point out " all the singular conclusions " which may be drawn therefrom.[2]

How many details he has enshrined in his interesting *Memoirs*, and how many facts we may glean from this great master ! He, like Fabre, had the gift of charming a great number of his contemporaries. Tremblay, Bonnet, and de Geer owed their vocations to Réaumur, not to speak of Huber, whose genius he inspired.

A physicist before all, and accustomed to delicate and meticulous though comparatively simple tasks, he had admirably foreseen the extraordinary complication of these inquiries ; so much so that, with the modesty of the true scientist that he was, he regarded his own studies, even the most substantial, as mere indications, intended to point the way to those that followed him.

As methodical, in short, as the author of the *Souvenirs*, the scrupulous Réaumur wrote nothing that he himself had not proved or verified with the greatest care ; and we may be sure that all that he records of his personal and immediate observations he has really seen with his own eyes.

In the wilderness of error he had, like Fabre, an infallible compass in his extraordinary common sense ; and, equally skilled in extracting from the false the little particle of truth which it often contains, he was no less fond of listening at the gate of legends, of tracing the source of traditions ; rightly considering that before deriding them as old-wives' tales we should first probe in all directions into their origin and foundation.3

He was also tempted to experiment, and he well knew that in such problems as those he attacked observation alone is often powerless to reveal anything. It is enough to recall here one of the most promising and unexpected of the discoveries which resulted from his experiments. Réaumur was the first to conceive the ingenious idea of retarding the hatching of insects' eggs by exposing them to cold, thus anticipating the application of cold to animal life and the discoveries of Charles Tellier, whose more illustrious forerunner he was ; at the same time he discovered the secret of prolonging, in a similar fashion, the larval existence of chrysalids during a space of time infinitely superior to that of their normal cycle ; and what is more, he succeeded in making them live a lethargic life for years and even for a long term of years, thus repeating at will the miracle of the Seven Sleepers.4

Too much occupied, however, with the smaller aspect of things, he had not the art of forcing Nature to speak, and in the province of psychical aptitudes he was barely able to rise above the facts.

As he was powerless to enter into real communion with the tiny creatures which he observed, although his observations were conducted with religious admiration; as he saw always only the outside of things, like a physicist rather than a poet or psychologist, he contented himself with noting the functioning of their organs, their methods of work, their properties, and the changes which they undergo; he did not interpret their actions. The mystery of the life which quivers within and around them eludes him.. This is why his books are such dry reading. He is like a bright garden full of rare plants; but it is a monotonous garden, without life or art, without distant vistas or wide perspectives. His works are somewhat diffuse and full of repetitions; entire monographs, almost whole volumes, are devoted to describing the emerging of a butterfly; but they form part of the library of the curious lover of nature; they are consulted with interest, and will always be referred to, but it cannot be said that they are read.

After Réaumur, according to the dictum of the great Latreille, entomology was confined to a wearisome and interminable nomenclature, and if we except the Hubers, two unparalleled observers, although limited and circumscribed, the only writer who filled the interregnum between Réaumur and Fabre was Léon Dufour.

In the quiet little town whither he went to succeed his father, this military surgeon, turned country doctor, lived a busy and useful life.

While occupied with his humble patients, whom he preferred to regard merely as an interesting clinic, and while keeping the daily record of his medical observations, he felt irresistibly drawn " to ferret in all the holes and corners of the soil, to turn over every stone, large or small ; to shrink from no fatigue, no difficulty ; to scale the highest peaks, the steepest cliffs, to brave a thousand dangers, in order to discover an insect or a plant.[5]

A disciple of Latreille, he shone above all as an impassioned descriptive writer.

No one was more skilled in determining a species, in dissecting the head of a fly or the entrails of a grub, and no spectacle in the world was for him so fascinating as the triple life of the insect ; those magical metamorphoses, which he justly considered as one of the most astonishing phenomena in creation.[6]

He saw further than Réaumur, and burned with the same fire as Fabre, for he also had the makings of a great poet. His curiosity had assembled enormous collections, but he considered, as Fabre considered, that collecting is " only the barren contemplation of a vast ossuary which speaks only to the eyes, and not to the mind or imagination," and that the true history of insects should be that of their habits, their industries, their battles, their loves, and their private and social life ; that one must " search everywhere, on the ground, under the soil, in the waters, in the air, under the bark of trees, in the depth of the woods, in the sands of the desert, and even on and in the bodies of animals."

Was not this in reality the ambitious programme which Fabre was later to propose to himself when he entered into his Harmas and founded his living laboratory of entomology ; he also having set himself as his exclusive object the study of " the instincts, the habits of life, the labours, the struggles and the propagation of this little world, which agriculture and philosophy should closely consider "? 7

Dufour also had admirably grasped the place of the insect in the general harmony of the universe, and he clearly perceived that parasitism, that imbrication of mutually usurping lives, is "a law of equilibration, whose object is to set a limit to the excessive multiplication of individuals of the same type," that the parasites are predestined to an imprescriptible mission, and that this mysterious law " defies all explanation."

On the other hand, he did not become very intimate with these tiny peoples; his attention was dispersed over too many points; perhaps he was fundamentally incapable of concentrating himself for a long period upon a circumscribed object; perhaps he lacked that first condition of genius, patience, so essential to such researches : although he enriched science by an infinite multitude of precious facts and has recorded a quantity of details concerning the habits of insects, he did not succeed in representing any one of these innumerable little minds. He had an intense feeling for nature, but he was not able to interpret it, and his immense volume of work, scattered through nearly three hundred monographs, remains ineffective.

Let us compare with his work the vast epic of the *Souvenirs*. We become familiar with the whole life of the least insect, and all its unending related circumstances; we obtain sudden glimpses of insight into our own organization, with its abysses and its lacunæ, and also into those rich provinces or faculties which we are only beginning to suspect in the depths of our unconscious activity.

In the evening twilight, after the vast andante of the cicadæ is hushed, at the hour when the shining glow-worms " light their blue fires," and the " pale Italian cricket, delirious with its nocturnal madness, chirrups among the rosemary thickets," while in the distance sounds the melodious tinkle of the bell-ringer frogs, replying from one hiding-place to another, the old master shows us that profound and mysterious magic with which matter is endowed by the faintest glimmer of life.

He shows us the intimate connection of things, the universal harmony which so intimately allies all creatures ; and he shows us also that everywhere and all around us, in the smallest object, poetry exists like a hidden flame, if only we know how to seek it.

And in revealing so many marvellous energies in even the lowest creatures, he helps us to divine the infinity of phenomena still unguessed-at, which the subtlety of the unknowable force which thrills through the whole universe hides from us under the most trivial appearances.

For he has not told everything; this incommensurable region, which had hitherto remained unworked, is far from being exhausted.

How many unknown and hidden things are still left to be gleaned! There will be a harvest for all. Remember that "even the humblest species either has no history, or the little that has been written concerning it calls for serious revision"[8]; that a single bush, such as the bramble, suffices to rear more than fifty species of insects, and that each species, according to the just observation of Réaumur, "has its habits, its tricks of cunning, its customs, its industries, its art, its architecture, its different instincts, and its individual genius."

What a stupendous alphabet to decipher, of which we have as yet only commenced to read the first few letters! When we are able to read it almost entirely, when observers are more numerous and have concerted their efforts, mutually illuminating, completing and correcting one another, then, and then only, we shall succeed, if not in resolving some of those high problems which have never ceased to interest mankind, at least in seizing some reflected knowledge of ourselves, and in seeing a little farther into the kingdom of the mind.

XV

THE EVENINGS AT SÉRIGNAN

BUT it will doubtless be long before a new Fabre will resume, with the same heroic ardour, the life of solitary labour, varied only by a few austere recreations.

Rising at six o'clock, he would first of all pace the tiles of his kitchen, breakfast in hand ; so imperious in him was the need of action, if his mind was to work successfully, that even at this moment of morning meditation his body must already be in movement. Then, after many turns among the bushes of the enclosure, all irised with drops of dew which were already evaporating, he went straight to his cell : that is, to the silence of his laboratory.

There, in unsociable silence, invisible to all, he worked hard and steadily until noon ; pursuing an observation or carrying out some experiment, or recording what he saw or what he had seen the day before, or re-drafting his records in their final form.

How many who have come hither to knock
upon the door in these morning hours, or to ring
at the little gate, silent as the tomb, which gives
upon the private path frequented only by foot-
passengers on their way to the fields, have undertaken a fruitless journey ! But without such
discipline would it have been possible to accomplish such a task as his?

At last he would leave his workroom ; jaded,
exhausted by the excessive intensity of his work,
"face pale and features drawn." [1]

Now he is " at leisure : the half-day is over " ; [2]
and he can satisfy his immense need not of
repose, but of relaxation and distraction in less
severe occupations ; for he is never at any time
nor anywhere inactive ; incessantly making notes,
with little stumps of pencil which he carries
about in his pockets, and on the first scrap of
paper that comes to hand, of all that passes
through his mind. Those eternal afternoons,
which usually, in the depth of the French provinces, prove so dull and wearisome, seem short
enough to him. Now he will halt before his
plants, now stoop to the ground, the better to
observe a passing insect ; always in search of
some fresh subject of study ; or now bending
over his microscope.[3] Then he undertakes, for

his later-born children at Sérignan, the duties which he formerly performed for the elder family at Orange : he teaches them himself ; he has much to do with them, for their sake and for his own as well, for he is jealous of possessing them, and he regrets parting with them. They too have their tasks arranged in advance.

They are his assistants, his appointed collaborators, who keep and relieve guard, undertaking, in his absence, some observation already in hand, so that no detail may be lost, no incident of the story that unrolls itself sometimes with exasperating slowness beneath the bell-covers of the laboratory or on some bush in the garden. He inspires the whole household with the fire of his own genius, and all those about him are almost as interested as he.

At home, in the house, always wearing his eternal felt hat, and absorbed in meditation, he speaks little, holding that every word should have its object, and only employing a term when he has tested its weight and meaning. Silence at mealtimes again is a rule that no one of his household would infringe. But he unbends his brow when he receives a friend at his hospitable table, where but lately his smiling wife would sit, full of little attentions for him.4

Frugal in all respects, he barely touches the
dishes before him; avoiding all meats, and
saving himself wholly for the fruits; for is not
man naturally frugivorous, by his teeth, his
stomach, and his bowels? Certain dishes repel
him, for reasons of sentiment rather than through
any real disgust; such as *paté de foie gras,*
which reminds him too forcibly of the so cruelly
tortured goose : such cruelty is too high a price
to pay for a mere greasy mouthful.5   On the
other hand, he drinks wine with pleasure, the
harsh, rough " wine of the country " of the plains
of Sérignan.   He is also well able to appreciate
good things and appetizing cookery; no one
ever had a finer palate; but he is happiest in
seeing others appreciate the pleasures of the
table.   Witness that breakfast worthy of Gar-
gantua, which he himself organized in honour
of his guests, whom he had invited to an
excursion over the Ventoux Alp; where he seems
expressly to have commanded " that all should
come in shoals."   What a tinkling of bottles,
what piles of bread !   There are green olives
" flowing with brine," black olives " seasoned
with oil," sausages of Arles " with rosy flesh,
marbled with cubes of fat and whole pepper-
corns," legs of mutton stuffed with garlic " to
dull the keen edge of hunger "; chickens " to

amuse the molars "; melons of Cavaillon too, with white pulp, not forgetting those with orange pulp, and to crown the feast those little cheeses, so delightfully flavoured, peculiar to Mont Ventoux, " spiced with mountain herbs," which melt in the mouth.[6]

But his greatest pleasure is his pipe ; a briar, which in absence of mind he is always allowing to go out, and always relighting.

Respectful of all traditions, he has kept up the observance of old customs ; no Christmas Eve has ever been passed under the roof of his Harmas without the consecrated meats upon the table ; the heart of celery, the nougat of almonds, the dish of snails, and the savoury-smelling turkey. Then, stuck into the Christmas bread,[7] the sprigs of holly, the *verbouisset,* the sacred bush whose little starry flowers and coral berries, growing amid evergreen leaves, affirm the eternal rebirth of indestructible nature.

At Sérignan Fabre is little known and little appreciated. To tell the truth, folk regard him as eccentric ; they have often surprised him in the country lying on his stomach in the middle of a field, or kneeling on the ground, a magnifying glass in hand, observing a fly or some one of those insignificant creatures in which no sane person would deign to be interested.

How should they know him, since he never goes into the village? When he did once venture thither to visit his friend Charrasse, the schoolmaster, his appearance was an event of which every one had something to say, so greatly did it astonish the inhabitants.[8]

Yet he never hesitates to place his knowledge at the service of all, and welcomes with courtesy the rare pilgrims in whom a genuine regard is visible, although he is always careful never to make them feel his own superiority; but he very quickly dismisses, sometimes a trifle hastily, those who are merely indiscreet or importunate; pedantic and ignorant persons he judges instantaneously with his piercing eyes; with such people he cannot emerge from his slightly gloomy reserve; he shuts himself up like the snail, which, annoyed by some displeasing object, retires into its shell, and remains silent in their presence.

Professors come to consult him: asking his advice as to their programmes of instruction, or begging him to resolve some difficult problem or decide some especially vexed question; and his explanations are so simple, so clear, so logical that they are astonished at their own lack of comprehension and their embarrassment.[9]

But there are few who venture within the walls

of that enclosure, which seems to shut out all
the temptations of the outer world ; the only intimate visitors to the Harmas are the village schoolmaster—first Laurent, then Louis Charrasse,[10]
and later Jullian—and a blind man, Marius.

This latter lost his sight at the age of twenty.
Then, to earn a living, he began to make and
repair chairs, and in his misfortune, although
blind and extremely poor, he kept a calm and
contented mind.

Fabre had discovered the sage and the blind
man on his arrival at Sérignan, and also
Favier,[11] "that other native, whose jovial spirit
was so prompt to respond, and who helped to
dig up the Harmas ; to set up the planks and
tiles of the little kitchen-garden ; a rude task,
since this scrap of uncultivated ground was
then but a terrible desert of pebbles." To
Favier fell the care of the flowers, for the new
owner was a great lover of flowers. Potted
plants, sometimes of rare species, were already,
as to-day, crowded in rows upon the terrace
before the house, where all the summer they
formed a sort of vestibule in the open air, on
either side of the entrance ; and these Fabre
never ceased to watch over with constant and
meticulous care. Both spoke the same language,
and the words they exchanged were born of a

like philosophy ; for Favier also loved nature in his own way, and at heart was an artist ; and when, after the day's work, sitting " on the high stone of the kitchen hearth, where round logs of green oak were blazing," he would evoke, in his picturesque and figurative language, the memories of an old campaigner, he charmed all the household and the evening seemed to pass with strange rapidity.

When this precious servant and boon companion had disappeared, after two years of digging, sowing, weeding, and hoeing, all was ready ; the frame was completed and the work could be commenced. It was then that Marius became the master's appointed collaborator, and it is he who now constructs his apparatus, his experimental cages ; stuffs his birds, helps to ransack the soil, and shades him with an umbrella while he watches under the burning sun. Marius cannot see, but so intimate is his communion with his master, so keen his enthusiasm for all that Fabre does, that he follows in his mind's eye, and as though he could actually see them, all the doings at which he assists, and whose inward reflection lights up his wondering countenance.

Marius was not only rich in feeling and the gift of inner vision ; he had also a marvellously correct ear. He was a member of the *Fanfare* of Sérignan, in which he played the big drum, and there was no one like him for keeping perfect time and for bringing out the clash of the cymbals.

Charrasse was no less fervent a disciple; he worshipped science and all beautiful things; and he could even conceive a noble passion for his exhausting trade of school-teaching.

Like Marius, he ate "a bitter bread"; and Fabre would get on with them all the better in that they, like himself, had lived a difficult life. "Man is like the medlar," he liked to tell them; "he is worth nothing until he has ripened a long time in the attic, on the straw."

> "L'homme est comme la nèfle, il n'est rien qui vaille
> S'il n'a mûri longtemps, au grenier, sur la paille."

These humble companions afforded him the simple conversation which he likes so well; so natural, and so full of sympathy and common sense. They customarily spent Thursday and Sunday afternoons at the Harmas; but these beloved disciples might call at any hour; the master always welcomed them, even in the morning, even when he was entirely absorbed in his work and could not bear any one about him. They were his circle, his academy; he would read them the last chapter written in the morning ; he shared his latest discoveries with them ; he did not fear to ask advice of their " fertile ignorance." [12]

Charrasse was a " Félibre," versed in all the secrets of the Provençal idiom, of which he knew all the popular terms, the typical expressions and turns of speech ; and Fabre loved to consult him, to read some charming verses which he had just discovered, or to recite some delightful rustic poem with which he had just been inspired ; for in such occupations he found one of his favourite relaxations, giving free vent to his fancy, a loose rein to the poet that dwells within him. These poems the piety of his brother has preserved in the collection entitled *Oubreto.* It is at such a moment that one should see his black eyes, full of fire ; his power of mimicry and expression, his impassioned features, lit up by inspiration, truly idealized, almost transfigured, are at such times a thing to be remembered.

Sometimes, again, in the shadow of the planes, on summer afternoons, when the cigales were falling silent ; or in the winter, before the blazing fireplace, in that dining-room on the ground floor in which he welcomed his visitors ; when out of doors the mistral was roaring and raging, or the rain clattering on the panes, the little circle was enlarged by certain new-comers, his nephews, nieces, a few intimates, of whom, a little later, I myself was often one. At such times his humour and imagination were given full play, and it was truly a rare pleasure to sit there, sipping a glass of mulled wine, during those delightful and earnest hours ; to taste the charm of his smiling philosophy, his picturesque conversation, full of exact ideas, all the more profound in that they were founded on experience and pointed or adorned by proverbs, adages, and anecdotes. Thanks to the daily reading of the *Temps,* which one of his friends regularly sends him, Fabre is in touch with all the ideas of the day, and expresses his judgment of them ; for example, he does not conceal his scepticism with regard to certain modern inventions, such as the aeroplane, whose novelty rather disturbs his mind, and whose practical bearing seems to him to be on the whole somewhat limited.

Thus even the most recent incidents find their way into the solitude of the Harmas and help to sustain the conversation.

" The first time we resume our Sérignan evenings," he wrote to his nephew on the morrow of one of these intimate gatherings, " we will have a little chat about your Justinian, whom the recent drama of *Théodora* has just made the

fashion. Do you know the history of that
terrible hussy and her stupid husband? Perhaps
not entirely; it is a treat I am keeping for
you." [13]

The only subject which is hardly ever mentioned during these evenings at Sérignan is
politics, although Fabre, strange as it may seem,
was one year appointed to sit on the municipal
council.

The son of peasants, who has emerged from
the people yet has always remained a peasant,
has too keen a sense of injustice not to be a
democrat; and how many young men has he
not taught to emancipate themselves by knowledge? But above all he is proud of being a
Frenchman; his mind, so lucid, so logical, which
has never gone abroad in search of its own
inspirations, and has never been influenced by
any but those old French masters, François
Dufour and Réaumur, and the old French
classics, has always felt an instinctive repugnance, which it has never been able to overcome,
for all those ideas which some are surreptitiously
seeking to put forward in our midst in favour
of some foreign trade-mark.

Although his visit to the court of Napoleon III.
left him with a rather sympathetic idea of the
Emperor, whose gentle, dreamy appearance he

still likes to recall, he detested the Empire and the " brigand's trick " which established it.

On the day of the proclamation of the Republic he was seen in the streets of Avignon in company with some of his pupils. He was agreeably surprised at the turn events had taken, and delighted by the unforeseen result of the war.

A spirit as proud and independent as his was naturally the enemy of any species of servitude. State socialism of the equalitarian and communistic kind was to him no less horrifying. Was not Nature at hand, always to remind him of her eternal lessons?

" Equality, a magnificent political label, but scarcely more ! Where is it, this equality? In our societies shall we find even two persons exactly equal in vigour, health, intelligence, capacity for work, foresight, and so many other gifts which are the great factors of prosperity? . . . A single note does not make a harmony : we must have dissimilar notes ; discords even, which, by their harshness, give value to the concords ; human societies are harmonious only thus, by the concourse of dissimilarities." [14]

And what a puerile Utopia, what a disappointing illusion is that of communism ! Let us see under what conditions, at the price of what sacrifices, nature here and there realizes it.

Among the bees " twenty thousand renounce maternity and devote themselves to celibacy to raise the prodigious family of a single mother."

Among the ants, the wasps, the termites " thousands and thousands remain incomplete and become humble auxiliaries of a few who are sexually gifted."

Would you by chance reduce man to the life of the Processional caterpillars, content to nibble the pine-needles among which they live, and which, satisfied to march continually along the same tracks, find within reach an abundant, easy, and idle subsistence?   All have the same size, the same strength, the same aptitudes.   No initiative.   " What one does the others do, with equal zeal, neither better nor worse."   On the other hand, there is " no sex, no love."   And what would be a society in which there was no work done for pleasure and from which love and the family were banished?   What would be the effect upon its progress, its welfare, its happiness?   Would not all that make the charm of life disappear for good?   However imperfect our present society may be, however mysterious its destinies, it is not in socialism that Fabre foresees the perfection of future humanity, for to him the true humanity does not as yet exist; it is making its way, it is slowly progressing, and in this evolution he wishes with all his heart to believe. Modern humanity is as yet only a shapeless grimacing caricature, and its life is like a play written by madmen and played by drunken actors; according to those profound words of the great poet, with which his mind is in some sort imbued; which he often repeats, and which he has transcribed at the head of one of his last records as an epigraph and a constant reminder.

And you who groan over the distressing problem of depopulation, lend an ear to the lesson of the Copris, " which trebles its customary batch of offspring in times of abundance, and in times of dearth imitates the artisan of the city who has only just enough to live on, or the *bourgeois,* whose numerous wants are more and more costly to satisfy, limiting the number of its offspring lest they should go in want, often reducing the number of its children to a single one." [15]

Instead of running after so many false appearances and false pleasures, learn to return to simpler tastes, to more rustic manners; free yourselves from a mass of factitious needs; steep yourself anew in the antique sobriety, whose desires were sager; return to the fields, the source of abundance, and the earth, the eternal foster-mother!

And in this appeal to return to nature, which perhaps since the time of Rousseau has never been worded so eloquently, Fabre has in view if not the strong, the predestined, who are called elsewhere, and who are actuated by the sense of great tasks to be performed, at least all those of rural origin, all those for whom the love of the family, the daily task, and a peaceful heart are really the great things of life, the things that count, the things that suffice.

He himself, although he was one of the strong, did not care to break any of the ties that bound him to his origins. Like the Osmia, " which retains a tenacious memory of its home," the beloved village of his childhood has never been effaced from his memory, and for a long time the desire to leave his bones there haunted him. His mind often returned to it ; he thought that there, better than anywhere else, he would find peace ; that it would please him to wander among the rocks, the trees, the stones which he had so loved, in the old days, and that all these things would recognize him too.

One day, however, when I was begging him to make up his mind on this point—it was one of those peaceful evenings which are troubled under the plane-trees only by the tinkling of the fountain—he confided to me that his beloved

Sérignan had at last, in his secret preferences, obliterated the old longing. As he advanced in life, in fact, although he never forgot his rude natal countryside, he felt that new links were daily binding him more closely to those heaths and mountains on which his heart had been so often thrilled with the intense joy of discovery, and that it was indeed in this soil, to him so full of delight, amid its beautiful hymenoptera and scarabæi, that he would wish to be buried.

Fabre is by no means the misanthrope that some have chosen to think him. He delights in the society of women, and knows how to welcome them gracefully; and more than any one he is sensitive to the pleasant and stimulating impressions produced by the conversation of cultivated people.

He is no less fond of the arts, provided he finds in them a sincere interpretation of life. This is why the theatre, with its false values, its tinsel and affectation, has to him seemed a gross deformation of the reality, ever since the day when at Ajaccio he attended a performance of *Norma*, in which the moon was represented by a round transparent disc, lit from behind by a lantern hanging at the end of a string, whose oscillation revealed by turns first the luminary and then the transparency. This

was enough to disgust him for ever with the
theatre and the opera, whose motionless choruses,
contrasting with the sometimes frantic movement
of the music, left him with a memory of an insane
and illogical performance.

Nevertheless, he adored music, of which he
knew something, having learned it, as he learned
his drawing, without a master ; but he preferred
the naïve songs of the country, or the melody
of a flute, to the most scholarly concert-music.[16]
In the intimacy of the modest chamber which
serves as the family *salon*, with its few shabby
and old-fashioned pieces of furniture, he plays
on an indifferent harmonium little airs of his
own composition, the subjects of which were at
first suggested by his own poetry.   Like Rollinat,
Fabre rightly considers that music should complete, accentuate, and release that which poetry
has perforce left incomplete or indefinite.   This
is why he makes the *bise* laugh and sing and
roar ; why he imitates the organ-tones of the
wind in the pines, and seeks to reproduce some
of the innumerable rhythms of nature ; the
frenzy of the lizard, the wriggling of the stickle-
back, the jumping gait of the frog, the shrill
hum of the mosquito, the complaint of the
cricket, the moving of the Scarabæi, and the
flight of the Libellulæ.

Too busy by day to find time for much
reading, it was at night that he would shut himself up. Retiring early to his little chamber,
with bare walls and bare tile floor, and a window
opening to the garden, he would lie on his low
bed, with curtains of green serge, and would
often read far into the night.

This philosopher, to whose books the philosophers of the future will resort for new theories
and original ideas, refuses to have any commerce with other philosophers, disdaining their
systems and preferring to go straight to the facts.
Even when he took up Darwin's *Origin of Species*
he did little more than open the book ; so wearisome and uninteresting, he told me, did he find
the reading of it. On the other hand, he is full
of the ancient philosophers, and as he did not
read them very extensively in his youth and
middle age, he has returned to them finally with
love and predilection for " these good old
books." Unlike many thinkers of the day, he
is persuaded that we cannot with impunity dispense with classic studies ; and he rightly
considers that science and the humanities are
not rivals, but allies. Above all he has a
particular affection for Virgil ; one may say that
he is steeped in his poetry ; and he knows La
Fontaine by heart. The style of the latter is

curiously like his own, and Fabre owns himself as his disciple ; certainly La Fontaine's is
the most active influence which his work reveals.
He has a profound acquaintance with Rabelais,
who was always his " friend " and who constantly crops up in his conversation and his
chance remarks.

After these his intellectual foster-parents have
been Courrier, Toussenel, of whom he is passionately fond, and Rousseau, of whom he cares
for little but his *Lettres sur la botanique*, full
of such fresh impressions, in which we feel not
the literary man but the " craftsman " ; he also
cherishes Michelet ; so full of intuition, although
he never handled actual things and knew nothing
of the practice of the sciences ; not learned,
but overflowing with love ; his magic pen, his
powers of evocation, and his deft brushwork
delight Fabre, despite the poverty and insufficiency of his fundamental facts ; [17] sometimes
Michelet has been his inspiration. The two do
really resemble one another ; Michelet was no
less fitted than Fabre to play the confidant to
Nature, and his heart was of the same mettle.

Since I have spoken of his favourites, let me
also speak of his dislikes ; Racine, whom he
cannot bear ; Molière, whom he does not really
like ; Buffon, whom he frankly detests for his

too fluent prose, his ostentatious style, and his vain rhetoric. The only naturalist whom he might really have delighted in, had he possessed his works and been able to read them at leisure, is Audubon, the enthusiastic painter of the birds of America. In him he felt the presence of a mind and a temper almost identical with his own.

XVI

TWILIGHT

How he has laboured in this solitude! For he considers that he is still far from having completed his task. He feels more and more that he has scarcely done more than sketch the history of this singular and almost unknown world. "The more I go forward," he wrote to his brother in 1903, "the more clearly I see that I have struck my pick into an inexhaustible vein, well worthy of being exploited." [1]

What studies he has undertaken, what observations he has carried out, "almost at the same time, the same moment!" His laboratory is crowded with these subjects of experiments. "As though I had a long future before me "—he was then just eighty years old—" I continue indefatigably my researches into the lives of these little creatures." [2]

Work in solitude seems to him, more and more, the only life possible, and he cannot even imagine any other.

" The outer world scarcely tempts me at all ;
surrounded by my little family, it is enough for
me to go into the woods from time to time, to
listen to the fluting of the blackbirds. The very
idea of the town disgusts me. Henceforth it
would be impossible for me to live in the little
cage of a citizen, Here I am, run wild, and I
shall be so till the end." 3

For him work has become more than ever an
organic function, the true corollary of life.
" Away with repose ! For him who would
spend his life properly there is nothing like
work—so long as the machine will operate."

Is this not the great law for all creatures so
long as life lasts?

Why should the man who has made a fortune,
who has neither children nor relations, and who
may die to-morrow, continue to work for himself
alone, to employ his days and his energies in
useless labours which will profit neither himself
nor his kind?

Ask of the Halictus, which, no longer capable
of becoming a mother, makes herself guardian
of a city, in order still to labour within the
measure of her means.

Ask of the Osmia, the Megachile, the Anthidium, which " with no maternal aim, for the sole
joy of labour, strive to expend their forces in

the accomplishment of their vain tasks, until
the forces of life fail."

Ask of the bee, which inaction leaves passive
and melancholy so that she presently dies of
weariness ; of the Chalicodoma, so eager a
worker that she will " let herself be crushed
under the feet of the passer-by rather than
abandon her task."

Ask it of all nature, which knows neither halt
nor repose, and who, according to the profound
saying of Goethe " has pronounced her male-
diction upon all that retards or suspends her
progress."

Let us then labour, men and beasts, " so that
we may sleep in peace ; grubs and caterpillars
in that torpor which prepares them for the transformation into moths and butterflies, and ourselves in the supreme slumber which dissolves
life in order to renew it."

Let us work, in order to nourish within ourselves that divine intuition thanks to which we
leave our original impress upon nature ; let us
work, in order to bring our humble contribution
to the general harmony of things, by our painful and meritorious labour ; in order that we
may associate ourselves with God, share in His
creation, and embellish and adorn the earth and
fill it with wonders.[4]

Forward then ! always erect, even amid the
tombs, to forget our griefs. Fabre finds no better
consolation to offer his brother, who has lost
almost in succession his wife and his eldest
daughter :

" Do not take it ill if I have not condoled
with you on the subject of your recent losses.
Tried so often by the bitterness of domestic
grief, I know too well the inanity of such con-
solations to offer the like to my friends. Time
alone does a little cicatrize such wounds ; and,
let us add, work. Let us keep on our feet and
at work as long as we are able. I know no
better tonic." 5

And this exhortation to work, which recurs so
often in the first letters of his youth, was to be
the last word of the last volume which so splendidly terminates the incomparable series of his
Souvenirs: " Laboremus."

*   *   *   *   *

Age has killed neither his courage nor his
energies, and he continues to work with the
same zeal at nearly ninety years of age, and with
as much eagerness as though he were destined
to live for ever.

Although his physical forces are failing him,
although his limbs falter, his brain remains intact,
and is giving us its last fruit in his studies on

the Cabbage caterpillar and the Glow-worm, which mark a sudden rejuvenescence of thought on his part, and the commencement of a new cycle of studies, which promise to be of the greatest originality.

To him the animal world has always been full of dizzy surprises, and the insects led him " into a new and barely suspected region, which is *almost absurd*." [6]

The glow-worms, motionless on their twigs of thyme, light their lamps of an evening, in the cool of the beautiful summer nights. What do these fires signify? How explain the mystery of this phosphorescence? Why this slow combustion, " this species of respiration, more active than in the ordinary state "? and what is the oxidizable substance " which gives this white and gentle luminosity "? Is it a flame of love like that which lights the Agaric of the olive-tree " to celebrate its nuptials and the emission of its spores "? But what reason can the larva have for illuminating itself? Why is the egg, already enclosed in the secrecy of the ovaries, already luminous?

" The soft light of the Agaric has confounded our ideas of optics ; it does not refract, it does not form an image when passed through a lens, it does not affect ordinary photographic plates." [7]

But here are other miracles :

" Another fungus, the Clathrix, with no trace of phosphorescence, affects photographic plates almost as quickly as would a ray of sunlight. The *Clathrix tenebrosa* does what the *Agaricus olearius* has no power to do." [8]

And if the beacon of the Glow-worm recalls the light of the Agaric, the Clathrix reminds us of another insect, the Greater Peacock moth.

In the obscurity of a dark chamber this splendid moth emits phantasmal radiations, perhaps intermittent and reserved for the season of nuptials, signals invisible to us, and perceptible only to those children of the night, who may have found this means to communicate one with another, to call one another in the darkness, and to speak with one another.[9]

Such are the interesting subjects which only yesterday were occupying this great worker ; the occult properties, the radiant energies of organic matter ; of phosphorescence, of light, the living symbols of the great universal Eros.

But embarrassment long ago succeeded the ephemeral prosperity which marked the first years of his installation at Sérignan, and that period of plenty was followed by a period of difficulty, almost of indigence. His class-books,

which had succeeded marvellously, and from
which the royalties had quickly attained to nearly
£640, which was the average figure for nearly
ten years, were then no longer in vogue. Already
the times had changed. France was in the crisis
of the anti-clerical fever. Fabre made frequent
allusions in his books of a spiritual nature, and
many primary inspectors could not forgive what
they regarded as a blemish.

We must also mention the keen competition
caused by the appearance of similar books,
usually counterfeit, and the more harmful for
that ; and as their adoption depended entirely
on the caprice of commissions or the choice of
interested persons, those of Fabre were gradually
ceasing to sell.

It was from 1894 especially that their popularity declined so rapidly :

" Despite all my efforts here I am more
anxious than ever about the future," he wrote
to his publisher on the 27th of January, 1899;
" two more of my books are about to disappear,
a prelude to total shipwreck. . . . I begin to
despair." [10]

He was not the man to have saved much
money ; numerous charges were always im-
posing themselves on him, and his first wife,
careless of expenditure, had been somewhat
extravagant.

While his position as teacher deteriorated his
Souvenirs brought him little more than a nominal
profit ; for to most people he was still completely
unknown among the potentates who monopolize
the attention of the crowd.

" Work such as a Réaumur might be proud
of will leave me a beggar, that goes without
saying, but at least I shall have left my grain
of sand. I would long ago have given up in
despair, had I not, to give me courage, the continual research after truth in the little world
whose historian I have become. I am hoarding
ideas, and I make shift to live as I can." [11]

Yet his reputation had long ago crossed the
frontiers of his country. He had been a corresponding member of the Institute of France
since 1887, and a Petit d'Ormoy prizeman.[12]
He was a member of the most celebrated foreign
academies, and the entomological societies of the
chief capitals of Europe ; but his fame had not
passed the walls of these academies and the
narrow boundaries of the little world of pro-
fessional biologists and philosophers.

Even in these circles, where he was almost
exclusively read and appreciated, he was little
known, and although he was much admired,
although he was readily given credit for his

admirable talent and exceptional knowledge, his readers were far from realizing the real powers of this world of life which he has called into being. His books are of those whose fertilizing virtues remain long hidden, to shine only at a distance, when much frothy writing, that has made a sudden noise in its time, has fallen into oblivion.

Every two or three years, after much fond polishing, he would open the door to yet another volume which was ready to go forth ; adding astonishing chapters of the history of insects, wonderful fragments of animal psychology, but always obtaining only the same circumscribed success ; that is, exciting no public curiosity, and remaining unperceived in the midst of general indifference.

His books interested only a select class, who, it is true, welcomed them eagerly, and read them with wonder and delight. If they excited the curiosity of a few philosophers, of scientists and inquirers, and here and there determined a vocation, still more, perhaps, did they charm writers and poets ; they consoled Rostand at the end of a serious illness, their virtue, in some sort healing, procuring him both moral repose and a delightful relaxation.[13] For all these, we may say, he has been one of those ten or twelve

authors whom one would wish to take with one
into a long exile, were they reduced to choosing
no more before leaving civilization for ever.

Yet we must admit that this work has certain
undeniable faults. The title, in the first place,
has nothing alluring about it, and is calculated
to deter rather than to attract purchasers, by
evoking vague ideas of repulsive studies, too
arduous or too special.

People have no idea of the wonderful fairy-
land concealed by this unpopular title; no conception that these records are intended, not
merely for the scientist pure and simple, but in
reality for every one.

Moreover, the first few volumes were in no way
seductive. They boasted not the most elementary drawings to help the reader; not the
slightest woodcut to give a direct idea of the
insects described; of their shape, aspect, or
physiognomy; and a simple sketch, however
poor, is often worth more than long and
laborious descriptions. The first volumes especially, printed economically, at the least possible
expense, were not outwardly attractive.

It is also true that he had never founded any
great hopes on the sale of such works.

Very few people are really interested in the
lower animals, and Fabre has been reproached

with wasting his time over "childish histories, unworthy of serious attention and unlikely to make money," of wasting in frivolous occupations the time which is passing so quickly and can never return. And why should he have still further wasted so many precious hours in executing minute drawings whose reproduction would have involved an expenditure which his publisher would not dare to venture upon, and which he himself could not afford?

For this universal inquirer was well fitted for such a task, and all these creatures which he has depicted he is capable of representing with brush and pencil as faithfully as with his pen. He had it in him to be not only a writer, but an excellent draughtsman, and even a great painter. He has reproduced in water-colour, with loving care, the decorations of the specimens of prehistoric pottery which his excavations have revealed, and which he has endeavoured to reconstruct, with all the science of an archæologist. He has displayed the same skill in water-colour in that astonishing iconography, in which he has detailed, with marvellous accuracy, all the peculiarities of the mycological flora of the olive-growing districts.[14]

As for those "paltry figures" insufficient or flagrantly incorrect in drawing, with which many people are satisfied, he regards them as "intolerable" in his own books, and as absolutely contradicting the rigorous accuracy of his text.[15]

Of late years photography and the skill of his son Paul have supplied this deficiency. He taught his son to fix the insects on the sensitive plate in their true attitudes, in the reality of their most instantaneous gestures. However valuable such documents may be, how much we should prefer fine drawings, giving relief not only to forms and colours, but also to the most characteristic features and the whole living physiognomy of the creature ! This is the function of art ; but the great artist that was in Fabre was capable in this domain of rivalling the magical talent of an Audubon.

Such work was relinquished, although so many romances of nature, so much dishonest patchwork, won the applause due to success.

Fabre fell more and more into a state bordering on indigence, and finally he was quite forgotten. An opponent of evolution, he was out of the fashion. The encyclopædias barely mentioned him. Lamarckians and Darwinians, who still made so much noise in the world, ignored him ; and no one came now to open the gate behind which was ageing, in obscurity and deserted, " one of the loftiest and purest geniuses which the civilized world at that moment possessed; one of the most learned naturalists and one of the most marvellous of poets in the modern and truly legitimate sense of the word." [16]

In the department of Vaucluse, where he lived for more than sixty years, in Avignon itself, where he had taught for twenty years, the prefect Belleudy, who had succeeded in approaching him, was astonished and distressed to find " so great a mind so little known "; for even those about him scarcely knew his name. [17]

But what matter! The hermit of Sérignan was not discouraged; he was disturbed only by the failure of his strength, and the fear that he could not much longer exercise that divine faculty which had always consoled him for all his sorrows and his disappointments. He could scarcely drag his weary limbs across the pebbles of his Harmas; but he bore his eighty-seven years with a fine disdain for age and its failings, and although the fire of his glance and that whole, eager countenance still expressed his passion for the truth, his abrupt gestures, touched with irony, his simple bearing, and the extreme modesty of his whole person, spoke sufficiently of his pro-

found indifference toward outside contingencies,
for the baubles of fame and all the stupidities
of life.

At a few miles' distance, in another village,
that other great peasant, Mistral, the singer of
Provence, the poet of love and joy, the minstrel
of rustic labour and antique faiths, was pursuing,
amid the homage of his apotheosis, the incredible
cycle of his splendid existence.

This glory had come to him suddenly; this
fame " whose first glances are sweeter than the
fires of dawn," and which was never to desert
him for fifty long years.

The wind of favour which had sweetened his
youth continued to propel him in full sail. He
had only to show himself to be at once surrounded, felicitated, worshipped; and his mere
presence would sway a crowd as the black peaks
of the high cypresses are swayed by the great
wind that bears his name. Like Fabre, he had
remained faithful to his native soil; that soil
which the great naturalist had never been able
to leave without at once longing impatiently to
return to its dusty olives where the cigale sings,
its ilex trees and its thickets; and so he lived
far from the cities, in a quiet village, with the
same horizon of plains and hills that were

balmy with thyme, leading in his little home an equal life full of wisdom and simplicity.

The hermit of Sérignan was the Lucretius of this Provence, which had already found its Virgil. With a very different vision, each had the same rustic tastes, the same love of the free spaces of wild nature and the scenes of rural life. But Mistral, wherever he looked, saw human life as happy and simple, through the prism of his creative imagination and the optimism of his happy life. Fabre, on the contrary, behind the sombre realities which he studied, saw only the ferocious engagement of confused living forces, and a frightful tragedy.

Thus their two lives, which were like parallel lines, never meeting, were in keeping with their work. And while Mistral, still young and triumphant despite the years, was at Maillane overwhelmed with honours and consideration, the poor great man of Sérignan lived an obscure and inglorious existence.

He had the greatest trouble to live and rear his family, and almost his sole income consisted of an uncertain sum of £120 annually, which he had for some years received, in the guise of a pension, by the generosity of the Institute, as the Gegner prize.

Finally his situation was so precarious that he decided to sell to a museum that magnificent collection of water-colour plates in which he had represented, life-size and with an astonishing truth of colour, all the fungi which grow in Provence.

He wrote to Mistral on the subject, after the visit which the latter paid him in the spring of 1908 : the only visit of the kind. Before meeting in Saint-Estelle, the Paradise of the Félibres, they had wished not to die before at least meeting on this earth.

Fabre wrote to Mistral the following letter, which I owe to the kindness of the great poet :—

" I have never thought of profiting by my humble fungoid water-colours. . . . Fate will perhaps decide otherwise.

" In this connection, permit me to make a confession, to which your nobility of character encourages me. Until latterly I had lived modestly on the product of my school-books. To-day the weathercock has turned to another quarter, and my books no longer sell. So here I am, more than ever in the grip of that terrible problem of daily bread. If you think, then, that with your help and that of your friends my poor pictures might help me a little, I have decided to let them go, but not without bitterness. It

is like tearing off a piece of my skin, and I
still hold to this old skin, shabby as it may be ;
a little for my own sake, much more for my
family's, and much more again for the sake of
my entomological studies, studies which I feel
obliged to pursue, persuaded that for a long
time to come no one will care to resume them,
so ungrateful is the calling." [18]

At the instigation of the poet the prefect
Belleudy took it upon him to intercede with the
Minister, from whom he finally wrung a grant
of £40, " in encouragement of the sciences."
Finally he ventured to reveal the situation to the
General Council of Vaucluse, and to require it
to contribute at least its share, in order to ensure
a peaceful and decent old age to a man who
was not only the greatest celebrity of the department, but also one of the highest glories of the
nation. He pleaded so well and so nobly that
the assembly granted Fabre an annual sum of
£20, " as the public homage which his compatriots pay to his lofty science and *his excessive
modesty*." [19]   At the same time, in a generous
impulse, the Council placed at his disposal all
the scientific equipment of the departmental
laboratory of agricultural analysis, which was
no longer used ; there was indeed talk of
suppressing it.

Now that the burden of his days weighed so heavily on him, and his task was virtually finished, everything, by the customary irony of things, was coming his way simultaneously: not only what was necessary and indispensable, but even something that was superfluous.

So one day all these delicate instruments, useless to a biologist who by the very nature of his labours had done without them all his life, and had never wearied of denying their utility, arrived at Sérignan. He did not possess even one modest thermometer; and as for the superb microscope over which he so often bent, the only costly instrument in his rustic laboratory, it was a precious present which, at the instigation of Duruy, Dumas the chemist had given him years before; but a simple lens very often sufficed him. " The secrets of life," he somewhere writes, " are to be obtained by simple, makeshift, in-expensive means. What did the best results of my inquiry into instinct cost me? Only time, and above all, patience."

It was then that a few of his disciples, finally affected by such abandonment, decided to celebrate his jubilee, hoping thus to reveal both his name and his wonderful books to the crowd that knew nothing of him.[20]

It was time; a little longer, and, according to

his racy phrase, "the violins would have come too late." The old master is daily nearer his decline; his sight, once so piercing, is now so obscured that he can barely see to sign his name, in a small, tremulous hand, confused and illegible. His muscles are so feeble now that he can walk only in short steps, on his wife's arm, leaning on a cane; and he would soon be piteously exhausted were not some seat available within immediate reach. Very soon now he will no longer hope to make the tour of this Harmas, which his feet have trodden daily for thirty years. In this failure of the body all that survives are the two sparkling cavities of his eyes and his extraordinary memory.

But he is far from being mournful: he feels only an immense lassitude, and an infinite regret that perhaps he will not be able to bring his series of *Souvenirs* to the point he had desired; not wishing to die until he has pushed his career as far as is in his power; without having worked, on his feet, until the very hour when the light of this world is suddenly withdrawn, and his eyes open upon the infinite life, beyond the infinite worlds of space.

The festival took place on the 3rd of April of the year 1910, and was touching in its simplicity.

What an unforgettable day in the life of
Fabre! That morning the gate of the Harmas
was left open to all, and many of the people of
Sérignan who invaded the garden were able to
look for the first time on the face of their fellow-
citizen, who had so long lived among them, and
whom they had now, to their astonishment,
discovered.

But among the crowd of friends and admirers
who, coming from all parts, pressed around the
little pink house, the most amazed of all was
Marius, the blind cabinet-maker, unable to contain his intense delight at the sudden burning of
so much incense before his idol, for to him it
had seemed that this day of apotheosis would
never dawn!

For nothing was certain, although the day of
the jubilee had long been fixed. In the first
place there had been serious defections in the
ranks of the official personages who were to
take part in the ceremony. Then the weather
was terrible for the time of year; the spring had
commenced gloomily, a season of floods and
catastrophes. But on this morning the rain of
days had ceased to fall, and suddenly the sun
appeared.

Among other compliments and marks of
homage the old man was presented with a

golden plaque, on one side of which Sicard, who
stood revealed as a master of the burin, had
engraved his portrait with rare fidelity.   The
reverse was resplendent with one of the most
beautiful syntheses which the history of art has
known ; a surprising allegory, in which the
imagination of the artist evoked the man of
science, the singer of the insects, the landscape
which had seen the birth of so many little lives,
and the village amid the olive-trees, in front
of the sun-steeped Ventoux.

At this festival, the jubilee of a scientist,
the scientists were least numerous.

The banquet was given in the large room of
a café in the midst of Sérignan ; in order, no
doubt, that in this humble life even glory should
be modest.

As Fabre could not walk, he was helped into
the carriage of ceremony, which was sent
expressly from Orange, and the little procession,
which was swelled by the municipal choral
society, spurred on by Marius, moved slowly off
along the sole central street.

It was a great family repast : one of those
love-feasts in which all communicate in a single
thought.

Edmond Perrier brought the naturalist the
homage of the Institute, and expressed in un-

affected terms the just admiration which he himself felt. The better to praise him, he gave
a summary of his admirable career, and his
immortal work. At the evocation of this long
past of labour Fabre regretted his poor vanished
joys, " the sole moments of happiness in his life."

Moved to tears, by his memories and by the
simple and pious homage at last rendered to
his genius, he wept, and many, seeing him weep,
wept with him.

Others spoke in the name of the great anony-
mous crowd of friends, of all those who had
found a source of infinite enjoyment in his works.
At the same time the greatest writers, the greatest
poets sent on the same day, at the same hour,
their salutation or eloquent messages to the
" Virgil of the insects " [21] to the " good magician
who knew the language of the myriad little
creatures of the fields." [22]

Doubtless he would sooner or later have
received full justice ; but without this circumstance it is permissible to add that the end of
his life would have passed amidst the completest
oblivion, and that he would have taken leave
of the world without attracting any particular
attention. His death would have occurred unperceived, and when the little vault of Vaison
stone, up in the small square enclosure of pebbles

which serves as the village cemetery, where those
he has loved await him, came to be opened for
the last time, they would hardly have troubled
to close it again.

Yet the honours paid him were far from being
such as he merited.

Why, at this jubilee of the greatest of the
entomologists, was not a single appointed representative of entomology present? [22]

The fact is that the majority of those who
" amid the living seek only for corpses," according to the expression of Bacon, unwilling to see in
Fabre anything more than an imaginative writer,
and being themselves incapable of understanding
the beautiful and of distinguishing it in the true,
reproached him, perhaps with more jealousy than
conviction, with having introduced literature into
the domains of science.

Other entomological specialists accuse him of
presenting in the guise of science discoveries
which have been made by others.   But in the
first place, as he has read very little, he certainly did not know all that had been done by
others ; and what matter if he had discovered
nothing essential concerning this or that insect
if the result of his study of it has been to impreg-
nate it with something new, or to touch it with
the breath of life?

Others, finally, who wished to see with their own eyes the proof of his statements, have reproached him with a few errors ; but he observed so skilfully that these errors, if any have really slipped into his books, cannot be very serious.

He was one of the glories of the University, but it failed to add to the brilliance of this ceremony, and it is to be regretted that the Government could not amid its temporary preoccupations have done with all the spontaneity that might have been looked for the one thing which might on this memorable date have atoned for its unjust obliviousness. Since Duruy had created Fabre a chevalier of the Empire more than forty years had gone by, and in this long interval Fabre was absolutely ignored by the public authorities. While the State daily raises so many commonplace men to the highest honours, it was afterwards needful to procure the intervention of influential persons, to justify his worth and to prove his deserts, in order to obtain his promotion through one degree of rank in that Legion of Honour which his eminent services had so long adorned.

This tardy reparation at least had the result of shedding a twilight of glory over the evening of his life, and from that day he suddenly

appeared in his true place and took his rank as
a man of the first order. Everybody began to
read him, and presently no one was willing to
seem ignorant of him, for more of his *Souvenirs
entomologiques* were sold in a few months than
had been disposed of in more than twenty
years.[24]

At last Fabre experienced not only glory and
renown, but also popularity. This was only
justice, for his is essentially a popular genius.
Has he not striven all his life to place the marvels
of science within reach of all? And has he not
written above all for the children of the people?

So at last people have learned the way to the
Harmas; they go thither now in crowds, to visit
the enclosure and the modest laboratory, as to
a veritable place of pilgrimage which attracts
from afar many fervent admirers.

Some, it is true, go thither to see him simply
as an object of curiosity; but even among these
there are those who on returning thence, full of
enthusiasm for what they have seen, find the
flowers of the fields more sweet and fragile, and
the wild fragrance of the woods and hedges more
voluptuous, and the green of the trees more
tender. They have learnt to look at the earth
and to " kneel in the grass."

Scientists come to chat with the scientist.

Others come to salute the primary schoolman, the lay instructor, the great pedagogue whose glory is reflected upon all the primary schools of France.

Those who cannot visit him write, telling him of all the pleasure which they owe him, thanking him for long and delightful hours passed in the reading of his books, expressing the hope that he may yet live many years, and still further increase the number of his *Souvenirs*.

Some ask him a host of questions relating to entomology or philosophy; others ask him for impossible answers to some of the fascinating and mysterious problems which he has expounded; women confide in him their little private griefs or their intimate sorrows, a naïve form of homage; but a thousand times more touching than any other, and one that shows how profound has been the beneficent influence of his books upon certain isolated minds, and what consolation can be derived from science when it finds a sufficiently eloquent voice to interpret it.

As he can work no longer, these visits now fill his life, formally so occupied; and in the midst of all the sympathy extended to him he is sensible, not of the twilight, but of a sunrise; he feels that his work has been good, that an infinity of minds are learning through him to regard plants and animals with greater affection ; and that the consideration of men, finally directed upon his work, will not readily exhaust it, for it is one of the Bibles of Nature.

NOTES

INTRODUCTION

1. Letters to his brother, 1898–1900.

2. I have made some valuable " finds " here ; among other pieces cited the fragment on *Playthings*, the curious description of the *Eclipse*, and the poem on *Number* are here published for the first time.

3. This negligence in the matter of correspondence is not least among the causes which have mitigated against his popularity.

I

1. " It is a country that has very little charm." To his brother, 18th August, 1846.

2. *Praticien, homme d'affaires ou de chicane :* roughly, " practitioner, man of business or law " : so his father is described in his birth certificate.

3. *Souvenirs entomologiques*, 2nd series, chap. iv, and 7th series, chap. xix.

4. *Id.*, 8th series, chap. viii.

5. To his brother, 15th August, 1896.

6. *Id.* " As brothers, we are one only ; but in virtue of our different tastes we are two, and I am amused and interested where you might well be bored."

7. Frédéric Fabre, like his brother, an ex-scholar of the normal primary school of Vaucluse, was first of all teacher at Lapalud (Vaucluse), then professor in the communal college of Orange. He was director of the primary school attached to the normal school of Avignon, where he voluntarily retired from teaching in 1859. He then became, successively, secretary to the Chamber of Commerce of Avignon, director of the Vaucluse Docks, and finally director of the Crillon Canal, which position he still occupies (Dec., 1912).

8. *Souvenirs entomologiques*, 10th series, chap. ix.

9. Among his innumerable manuscripts I have found a vast number of little poems, which date from this period.

10. It was then that he gave up his position to his brother Frédéric, who had continually followed closely in his steps, and who in turn had just obtained the qualification of pupil-teacher and bursar (August, 1842).

11. *Souvenirs entomologiques*, 10th series, chap. xxi.

12. To his brother, 2nd and 9th of June, 1851.

II

1. *Souvenirs entomologiques*, 1st series, chap. xx, and 9th series, chap. xiii.

2. *Id.*, 6th series, chap. xxi.

3. To his brother, from Ajaccio, 10th June, 1850.

4. *Id., id.*

5. *Id.*, from Carpentras, 15th August, 1846.

6. *Id.*, from Ajaccio, 10th June, 1850.

7. *Id.*, from Carpentras, 15th August, 1846.

8. *Id., id.*

9. *Souvenirs entomologiques*, 1st series, chap. xiv.

10. To his brother, from Carpentras, 3rd Sept., 1848.

11. *Id.*, 8th Sept., 1848.

12. *Id.*, *id.*

13. *Id.*, 3rd Sept., 1848.

14. *Id.*, *id.*

15. Letter to the Rector of the Nîmes Academy, 29th Sept., 1848.

16. To his brother, 29th Sept., 1848.

III

1. To his father, from Ajaccio, 14th April, 1850.

2. To his brother, from Ajaccio, 1851.

3. To his brother, from Ajaccio, 9th June, 1851.

" I have set to work upon a conchology of Corsica, which I hope soon to publish."

4. The *Helix Raspaillii.*

5. To his brother, from Ajaccio, 10th June, 1850.

6. *Id.*, *id.*

7. *Souvenirs entomologiques*, 9th series, chap. xiv.

8. Number (Le Nombre—APIΘMOΣ), poem, Ajaccio, Sept., 1852.

9. To his brother, from Ajaccio, 2nd June, 1851.

10. *Id.*, 10th Oct., 1852, and *Souvenirs entomologiques*, 10th series, chap. xxi.

11. Fr. Mistral, *Mémoires.*

Moquin-Tandon, born at Montpellier, was professor of Natural History at Marseilles, at Toulouse, and in Paris.

12. To his brother, from Ajaccio, 10th Oct., 1852.

13. *Id.*

14. To his brother, from Carpentras, 3rd Dec., 1851.

" Our crossing was atrocious. Never have I seen so terrible a sea, and that the packet-boat was not broken up by the force of the waves must have been due to the fact that our time had not yet come. On two or three occasions I thought my last moment was at hand ; I leave you to imagine what a terrible experience I had. In ordinary weather the packet by which we travelled makes the voyage from Ajaccio to Marseilles in about eighteen hours ; it is said to be the fastest steamer on the Mediterranean. On this occasion it took three days and two nights."

15. January, 1853.

IV

1. To his brother, from Avignon, 1st August, 1854.

"I have arrived at Toulouse, where I have passed the best examination one could possibly wish. I have been accepted as licentiate with the most flattering compliments, and the expenses of the examination should be returned to me. The examination was of a higher level than I had expected."

2. To M. —— (of the Institute), from Avignon, 1854.

(Letter communicated to M. Belleudy, prefect of Vaucluse, by M. Vollon, painter.)

3. *Id.*

4. To his brother, from Ajaccio, 10th Oct., 1852.

5. Observations concerning the habits of the Cerceris and the cause of the long preservation of the coleoptera with which it provisions its larvæ.—*Annales de Sc. natur.*, 4th series, 1855.

6. *Souvenirs entomologiques,* 10th series, chap. xxii.

7. "I had only one idea: to free myself, to leave the *lycée*, where, not being a fellow, I was treated as a subordinate. An inspector-general told me frankly one day, 'You will never amount to anything if you are not a

fellow' (*agrégé*). 'These distinctions disgust me,' I replied." (Conversations.)

8. To his brother, from Ajaccio, 14th Jan., 1850.

9. Inquiries respecting the tubercles of *Himantoglossum hircinum.* Thesis in Botany, 1855.

10. Inquiries respecting the anatomy of the reproductive organs, and the developments of the Myriapoda. Thesis in Zoology, 1855.

11. Prize for experimental physiology, 1856.

12. Letter to Léon Dufour, 1st Feb., 1857.

13. *The Origin of Species,* 1857, translated by Barbier, p. 15.

14. *Souvenirs entomologiques,* 1st series, chap. i, and 5th series, chap. i.

15. *Id.,* 1st series, chap. xvi.

16. *Id.,* 1st series, chap. i.

17. Henry Devillario, magistrate at Carpentras, where he performed his duties as *juge d'instruction* until his death. A notable collector and distinguished publicist.

Dr. Bordone, to-day at Frontignan. Vayssières, professor of Zoology in the faculty of sciences at Marseilles.

18. *Souvenirs entomologiques,* 1st series, chap. xiii.

19. He was subject in his youth to violent headaches, " which sometimes developed into a cerebral fever," as well as strange nervous troubles : " A few days ago I was attacked, at night, with a sudden nervous illness, of a terrifying nature, which I have not as yet been able to identify." To his brother, 3rd Sept., 1848.

Severe disappointment or annoyance always had a great effect upon him ; on the occasion of his first marriage he fell into a sort of cataleptic condition as a result of the opposition of his parents and relations, who sought to oppose it. (Conversations with his brother.)

20. *Souvenirs entomologiques*, 9th series, chap. xxiii.

21. *Id.*, 10th series, chap. xxii.

22. Letter to Léon Dufour, 1st Feb., 1857.

"Steps have been taken to obtain for me the post of drawing-master (*maître des travaux graphiques*). If they succeed, thanks to the little talent I have for drawing, my salary will reach a reasonable figure, £120, and I can then, by giving up these abominable private lessons, cultivate rather more seriously the studies into which you have initiated me." Communicated by M. Achard.

23. *Souvenirs entomologiques*, 10th series, chap. xxii.

24. Oubreto Prouvençalo. La Cigale et la Fourmi.

25. Lavisse. A minister. Victor Duruy.

26. Letter to the municipal councillors of Avignon.

27. J. Stuart Mill, *Autobiography*, chap. vi.

28. I have visited this house; nothing, at all events outside, has changed in the least.

29. Mill collaborated in his *Flore du Vaucluse* : "A virtuous man whose recent loss we shall all deplore joined his efforts to mine in this undertaking." Letter to the Mayor of Avignon, 1st Dec., 1833, communicated by M. Félix Achard.

V

1. *Chimie agricole.*

2. *Le Ciel.* Lectures et Leçons pour tous.

3. *La Terre.* Lectures et Leçons pour tous.

4. *La Chimie de l'oncle Paul.* Lectures courantes pour toutes les écoles.

5. *Histoire de la bûche.*

6. *Les jouets.* *Le Toton* (manuscript).

The primitive fountain, the "antique appliance" transmitted by inheritance, "the invention perhaps of some little unemployed herd-boy," consisted originally of three apertures and three straws ; two similar apertures on one side, with two short straws, which dipped into the water, and a single orifice on the other side for the longer straw which delivered the water. Happening one day to use only two straws, one on each side, the little Fabre perceived that the device worked just as well, and "so, quite unconsciously, without thinking of it, I discovered the syphon, the true syphon of the physicist." *Loco cit.*

7. " The chemistry course is a great success at home." To his brother, from Orange, 1875.

8. To his son Émile, 4th Nov., 1879.

" The household ; discussions as to domestic economy for use in girls' schools."

9. *Souvenirs entomologiques*, 2nd series, chap. i.

10. To the Mayor of Avignon, 1st Dec., 1873. Communicated by M. Félix Achard.

11. Letter to his brother, 1875.

12. *Id.*

VI

1. *Souvenirs entomologiques*, 2nd series, chap. i. *L'Harmas.*

2. *Id.*, 6th series, chap. v.

3. The *Lumbricus phosphoreus* of Dugés. Fabre had already clearly perceived that this curious phenomenon of phosphorescence appears at birth, and he saw in it a process of oxidation, a species of respiration, especially active in certain tissues.

Letter to Léon Dufour, 1st Feb., 1857. Communicated by M. Félix Achard.

4. To his brother, from Carpentras, 15th Aug., 1846.

5. He died at the age of 96.

6. *Souvenirs entomologiques,* 1st series, chap. xxi.

7. To his son Émile, 4th Nov., 1879.

8. To Henry Devillario, 30th March, 1883.

9. *Id.,* 17th Dec., 1888.

VII

1. *Souvenirs entomologiques,* 8th series, chap. xii.

2. *Id.,* 7th series, chap. xvi.

3. *Id.,* 1st series, chap. iv.

4. *Id.,* 2nd series, chap. iii.

5. *Id.,* 6th series, chap. xxi.

6. *Id.,* 1st series, chap. xix, and 2nd series, chap. vii.

7. *Id.,* 7th series, chap. xxiii.

8. Maeterlinck, *The Bee.*

9. *Souvenirs entomologiques,* 7th series, chap. ii.

10. *Id.,* 8th series, chap. xxii.

11. *Id.,* 6th series, chap. vi.

12. *Id.,* 9th series, chap. x.

13. Bergson, *l'Evolution créatrice.*

14. *Souvenirs entomologiques,* 10th series, chap. vi.

15. *Les Serviteurs* and *Les Auxiliaires.*

16. François Raspail, born at Carpentras in 1794, was also a professor at the college of Carpentras.

17. To his brother, 3rd Sept., 1848.

The improvement did not last long; the child died finally a short time afterwards.

18. *Souvenirs entomologiques,* 10th series, chap. xxi.

19. Ed. Perrier.   Private letter, 27th Oct., 1909.

" He is the finest of all our observers, and all scientists should bow to the facts which he excels in discovering."

20. *Souvenirs entomologiques,* 6th series, chap. xxv.

21. *Id.*, 10th series, chap. xvi.

22. *Id.*, 10th series, chap. xx.

23. Manuscripts, unpublished observations.

24. A common spectacle in Provence, but one which Fabre never wearied of seeing.

25. *Souvenirs entomologiques*, 6th series, chap. xvii.

26. We know that the great naturalist was far from being charmed by the song of the nightingale.

27. Manuscripts, unpublished observation. These remarks deal with the solar eclipse of 28th May, 1900.

28. Among the insects which he has observed there are many which are not always sufficiently characterized. *Insectes coléoptères observes aux environs d'Avignon.* Avignon, pub. Seguin, 1870.

29. Coleoptera observed in the neighbourhood of Avignon. A catalogue now very scarce, a copy of which I owe to the kindness of Dr. Chobaut, of Avignon.

30. *Nomina si nescis, perit et cognitio rerum.*

31. *Souvenirs entomologiques*, 4th series, chap. xi.

32. *Id.*, 9th series, chap. xix.

33. *Id.*, 1st series, chap. ix.

34. "Jenner's Legend of the isolation of the young Cuckoo in the nest," by Xavier Raspail, *Bull. de la Soc. Zool. de France*, 1903.

35. *Souvenirs entomologiques*, 1st series, *passim.*

36. *Id.*, 4th series, chap. xiv.

37. *Id.*, 1st series, chap. vii.

38. *Id.*, 2nd series, chap. ii.

VIII

1. *Souvenirs entomologiques*, 1st series, chap. ii.

2. Bergson, *l'Evolution créatrice.*

3. *Souvenirs entomologiques*, 2nd series, chap. iv.
4. *Id.*, 5th series, chap. viii.
5. *Id.*, 9th series, chap. iii.
6. *Id.*, 1st series, chap. xxii.
7. *Id.*, 4th series, chap. iii.
8. *Id.*, 4th series, chap. iii.
9. *Id.*, 4th and 1st series, chap. xix.
10. *Id.*, 9th series, chap. xxiv.
11. *Id.*, 10th series, chap. v.
12. *Id.*, 4th series, chap. vi.
13. *Id.*, 9th series, chap. xvi.
14. *Id.*, 2nd series, chap. v.
15. *Id.*, 5th series, chap. vii.
16. *Id.*, 6th series, chap. viii.
17. *Id.*, 3rd series, chaps. xvii, xviii. xix and xx.
18. *Id.*, 2nd series, chap. xv.
19. *Id.*, 3rd series, chap. xi.
20. Emerson.
21. *Souvenirs entomologiques*, 4th series, chap. ix.
22. Unpublished observations.
23. *Mireille*, 3rd canto.

IX

1. *Souvenirs entomologiques*, 8th series, chap. xxi.
2. *Les Ravageurs*, chap. xxxiv, agriculture.
3. *Souvenirs entomologiques*, 10th series, chap. xii.
4. *Id.*, 1st series, chap. ii., and 10th series, chap. xiii.
5. *Id.*, 2nd series, chap. xvii.
6. *Id.*, 7th series, chap. xx.
7. *Id.*, 2nd series, chap. iv.
8. *At novitas mundi nec frigora dura ciebat,*
   Nec nimios æstus.
   LUCRETIUS, *De Natura rerum.*

9. In this connection see the excellent introduction written by M. Edmond Perrier to serve as preface to the work of M. de Romanes : *l'Intelligence des animaux*.

10. *Souvenirs entomologiques*, 8th series, chap. xx.

11. To Henry Devillario, 30th March, 1883.

12. To Henry Devillario, 12th May, 1883.

13. To his brother, 1900.

14. Letters to his brother.

" I am not sulking; far from it . . . I have no lack of ink and paper ; I am too careful of them to lack them ; but I do lack time. . . . So you still think I am sulking because I do not reply ! But imagine, my dear and petulant brother, that for several weeks I have been pursuing, with unequalled persistence, some abominable conic problems proposed at the fellowship examination, and once I have mounted my hobby-horse, good-bye to letters, good-bye to replies, good-bye to everything." (Carpentras, 27th Nov. 1848.)

" You are right, seven times right to storm at me, to grumble at my silence, and I admit, in all contrition, that I am the worst correspondent you could find. To force myself to write a letter is to place myself on the rack, as well you know. . . . But why do you get it into your head, why do you tell me, that I disdain you, that I forget you, that I ignore you, you, my best friend ? . . . For my silence blame only the multiplicity of tasks, which often surpasses, not my courage, but my strength and my time." (Ajaccio, 1st June, 1851.)

15. *Souvenirs entomologiques*, 10th series, chap. viii.

16. *Id.*, 9th series, chap. ii.

X

1. *Souvenirs entomologiques*, 1st series, chap. xxi.
2. *Id.*, 9th series, chap. ii.
3. *Id.*, 10th series, chap. iv.
4. Montaigne's Essays.
5. *Souvenirs entomologiques*, 8th series, chap. xvii.
6. *Les Ravageurs.*
7. *Souvenirs entomologiques*, 10th series, chap. xviii, and *Merveilles de l'instinct*: *la Chenille du chou.*
8. *Id.*, 8th series, chap. xvii.

XI

1. *Souvenirs entomologiques*, 3rd series, chap. viii.
2. *Id.*, 2nd series, chap. xiv *et seq.*
3. *Id.*, 6th series, chap. ix.
4. *Id.*, 5th series, chap. xix.
5. Tolstoy : " All that the human heart contains of evil should disappear at the contact of nature, that most immediate expression of the beautiful and the good.' (*The Invaders.*)
6. The *Livre d'histoires* and *Chimie agricole.*
7. *Oubreto Prouvençalo. La Bise.*
8. *Id., Le Semeur.*
9. *Id., Le Crapaud.*

XII

1. *Oubreto Prouvençalo. Le Maréchal.*
2. *Oubreto Prouvençalo.*
3. In this connection see the admirable passage in Sainte-Beuve's *Port-Royal*, Book II, chap. xiv.
4. *Souvenirs entomologiques*, 4th series, chap. i.
5. *Id.*, 1st series, chap. xvii.

6. *Id.*, 7th series, chap. viii.

7. *Id.*, 7th series, chap. x.

8. *Id.*, 8th series, chap. viii.

9. *Id.*, 8th series, chap. xx.

10. *Id.*, 6th series, chap. xiv.

11. *Id.*, 8th series, chap. xviii.

12. *Id.*, 10th series, chap. viii.

13. *Id.*, 10th series, chap. vi.

14. *Id.*, 5th series, chap. xxii.

XIII

1. *Souvenirs entomologiques*, 10th series, chap. xvii.

2. *Id.*, 9th series, chap. iv, *l'Exode des araignées* (the Exodus of the Spiders), and chap. v, *l'Araignée crabe* (the Crab Spider).

3. *Id.*, 5th series, chap. xvii.

4. *Id.*, 3rd series, chap. xiii.

5. *Id.*, 6th series, chap. xiv.
   Oubreto. Le Grillon, and unpublished verses.

6. *Souvenirs entomologiques*, 2nd series, chap. xvi.

7. *Id.*, 9th series, chap. xxi.

8. *Les Merveilles de l'instinct: le Ver luisant* (Marvels of Instinct: the Glow-worm).

9. *Souvenirs entomologiques*, 2nd series, chap. xii.

10. *Id.*, 8th series, chap. xxii, and 9th series, chap. xi.

11. *Id.*, 5th series, chap. xviii.

XIV

1. Grandjean de Fouchy: eulogy of Réaumur, in *Recueils de l'Acad. des sciences*, vol. clvii H, p. 201, and Preface to the *Lettres inédites de Réaumur*, by G. Musset.

2. *Memories, passim,* and vol. ii, 1st *memoire.*

3. *Id.,* vol. iii, 3rd *mémoire.*

4. *Id.,* vol. ii, 1st *mémoire.*

Ch. Tellier, *Le Frigorifique* (Refrigeration), story of a modern invention, chap. xxiii; cold applied to the animal kingdom.

5. Léon Dufour : *Journal de sa vie.*

Souvenirs and impressions of travel in the Pyrenees to Gavarnie, Héas, the *Montagnes maudites,* etc. Entomological excursions on the dunes of Biscarosse and Arcachon.

6. *Id.,* direction of entomological studies.

7. *Souvenirs entomologiques,* 2nd series, chap. i : *L'Harmas.*

8. *Id.,* 5th series, chap. xi.

XV

1. Louis Charrasse, private letter, 20th Feb., 1912, and *Le Bassin du Rhône,* March, 1911.

2. *Oubreto. Le Crapaud.*

3. It was only in the afternoon that he devoted himself, when needful, to microscopic researches, on account of the better inclination of the light.

4. He lost it at the end of last spring.

5. *Les Serviteurs. Le Canard.*

6. *Souvenirs entomologiques,* 1st series, chap. xiii: an ascent of Mont Ventoux.

7. The name given to Christmas in Provence.

8. Louis Charrasse, private letters.

9. *Id.*

10. 1888–1892.

11. *Souvenirs entomologiques,* 2nd series, chap. ii.

12. Louis Charrasse, private letter.

13. Letter to his nephew, Antonin Fabre, 4th Jan., 1885.

14. *Souvenirs entomologiques*, 6th series, chap. xix.

15. *Id.*, 6th series, chap. ii.

16. *Id.*, 6th series, chap. xi.

17. Conversations.

XVI

1. Letter to his brother, 4th Feb., 1900.

2. To his brother, 18th July, 1908. At this time the eighth volume of his *Souvenirs* had just appeared, and the ninth was in hand.

3. *Id.*

4. *Chimie agricole.*

5. To his brother, 10th Oct., 1898.

6. Private letter, 30th March, 1908.

7. *Id.*

8. *Id.*

9. Unpublished experiments.

10. To Charles Delagrave, 27th Jan., 1899.

11. To his brother, 4th Feb., 1900.

12. This prize was awarded to Fabre in 1899. The amount of the prize is £400. It is one of the chief prizes of the Institute.

13. Edmond Rostand. Private letter, 7th April, 1910: " His books have been my delight during a very long convalescence."

14. This magnificent atlas, the gem of Fabre's collections, comprises nearly 700 plates, and a large body of explanatory and descriptive matter.

15. To Charles Delagrave, undated.

16. Maeterlinck. Private letter, 17th Nov., 1909.

"Les 4 Chemins,
"Grasse (Alpes-Maritimes).

"You overwhelm me with pleasure and do me the greatest honour in allowing my name to be inscribed among those of the committee which proposes to celebrate the jubilee of Henri Fabre. . . . Henri Fabre is, indeed, one of the chiefest and purest glories that the civilized world at present possesses; one of the most learned naturalists and the most wonderful of poets in the modern and truly legitimate sense of the word. I cannot tell you how delighted I am by the chance you offer me of expressing in this way one of the profoundest admirations of my life."

17. J. Belleudy, prefect of Vaucluse. Private letter, 29th Sept., 1909.

"It pains me to see so great a mind, so eminent a scientist, such a master of French literature, so little known. Two years ago, when the Gegner prize was awarded to him, I felt that I must speak of him to certain of those about me; and they had hardly heard his name!"

18. Letter to Frédéric Mistral, 4th July, 1908.

19. Council General of Vaucluse, session of August, 1908. The words of the recorder, M. Lacour, mayor of Orange, to-day deputy for Vaucluse, a personal friend and ardent admirer of the old master.

20. Edmond Rostand. Private letter, 20th Nov., 1909.

"I am, sir, not only greatly touched, but also and above all delighted that you have thought of including me among the friends who wish to fête Henri Fabre. Thanks for having considered that my name would assist your undertaking. The *Souvenirs entomologiques* have long ago made me intimate with his charming, profound, and moving genius. I owe them an infinity of delightful hours. Perhaps also I ought to thank them for having encouraged one of my sons to pursue the vocation which he entered. If, in order to honour Henri Fabre, you run the pious risk of disturbing, for a moment, the studious retreat in which, for so many years, he has pursued his life and his work, it is an act of justice toward this great scientist, who thinks as a philosopher, sees as an artist, and feels and expresses himself as a poet."

Romain Rolland. Private letter, 7th Jan., 1910.

"You cannot imagine what pleasure you have given me by requesting me to associate myself in the glorification of J. H. Fabre. He is one of the Frenchmen whom I most admire. The impassioned patience of his ingenious observations delights me as much as the masterpieces of art. For years I have read and loved his books. During my last holidays, of three volumes that I travelled with two were volumes of his *Souvenirs entomologiques*. You will honour me and delight me by counting me as one of you."

21. Edmond Rostand. Telegram.

22. Romain Rolland.

INDEX